Mastering the Alberta Trades Entrance Test: A Comprehensive Prep Guide

The "No-Nonsense" Alberta Trades Guide: Get In, Get Done, Get Working.

Complete
Test Preparation Inc.
WWW.TEST-PREPARATION.CA

Copyright 2026 Complete Test Preparation Inc. All Rights Reserved.

Intellectual Property Rights This publication is protected by copyright. No part of this book may be reproduced, copied, distributed, or transmitted in any form or by any means—including graphic, electronic, or mechanical methods such as photocopying, recording, or information storage and retrieval systems—without the prior written permission of the publisher, except in the case of brief quotations embodied in critical reviews and certain other noncommercial uses permitted by copyright law.

Disclaimer & Limitation of Liability While the publisher and author have used their best efforts in preparing this book, they make no representations or warranties with respect to the accuracy or completeness of the contents. The advice and strategies contained herein may not be suitable for your situation. Test content and administration rules change frequently; readers are advised to verify all information with the official test providers. Complete Test Preparation Inc. shall not be liable for any loss of profit or any other commercial damages, including but not limited to special, incidental, consequential, or other damages.

Non-Affiliation Notice Complete Test Preparation Inc. is an independent publisher and is not affiliated with, endorsed by, or sponsored by any testing organization, educational institution, or government agency mentioned in this publication. All trademarks, service marks, and trade names are the property of their respective owners and are used for reference and identification purposes only.

We strongly recommend that students check with exam providers for up-to-date information regarding test content.

Complete Test Preparation Inc. is not affiliated with the makers of the Alberta Trade Entrance Exam, who are not involved in the production of, and do not endorse this publication.

ISBN-13: 9781772454673
Version 10 March 2026

About Complete Test Preparation Inc.

Why Choose Complete Test Preparation? You want to spend your valuable study time where it counts the most. We've got you covered.

Since 2005, we have helped hundreds of thousands of students succeed with over 145 study guides and online courses. We know that tests change, which is why we keep our content current and relevant.

Study with a Purpose With this purchase, you are doing more than just preparing for a test. You are supporting a mission to improve education globally. We are proud to support charities that bring learning opportunities to those who need them most.

Learn more about our mission:
https://www.test-preparation.ca/charities-and-non-profits/

You have definitely come to the right place.
If you want to spend your valuable study time where it will help you the most - we've got you covered today and tomorrow.

Thank you for studying with us!

Feedback

We welcome your feedback. Email us at feedback@test-preparation.ca with your comments and suggestions. We carefully review all suggestions and often incorporate reader suggestions into upcoming versions. As a Print on Demand Publisher, we update our products frequently.

https://www.youtube.com/user/MrTestPreparation

CONTENTS

6   **Getting Started**
         How this study guide is organized   7
         Your 21-Day "Get-In-The-Trade" Game Plan   8

11   **Mastering Math**
         The Mathematics Self-Assessment   11
         Answer Key   20
         Basic Math Video Tutorials   22
         How to Answer Basic Math Multiple Choice   22
         Order Of Operation   25
         Converting Decimals to Fractions   26
         Percent Tips, Tricks and Short-cuts   27
         Fraction Tips, Tricks and Short-cuts   29
         Most Common Fraction Mistakes on a Test   36

37   **Trades Science - How Things Work**
         What's Under the Hood? (TEE Science Topics)   38
         Science Self-Assessment   41
         Answer Key   51
         Levers   55
         Pulleys: Multiplying Your Strength   58
         The Wedge: Splitting and Lifting   60
         The Screw: The Circular Ramp   61
         Gears and Gear Trains   63
         Basic Physics   65
         Understanding Energy   65
         Work and Power: Getting the Job Done   67
         Defining Force and Newton's Three Laws   70
         Friction: The Force That Holds Us Back   72
         Electromagnetism: Putting Electricity to Work   74
         Gravity: The Heavy Lifter   76
         The Four States of Matter   78
         Heat Transfer: The Three Ways Energy Moves   80
         The Golden Rule: Liquids Don't Squish   83
         Flashpoint: The "Match" Test   85

87	**The Launchpad: Reading**	
	Self-Assessment & Strategy	87
	Answers and Analysis	97
	The Bottom Line	103
	Reading Between the Lines	105
108	**English Essentials: Finding Your Starting Line**	
	Vocabulary & and Grammar Practice	112
	Answer Key & Analysis	117
	English Grammar and Punctuation Tutorials	119
	Capitalization: Making it Look Professional	119
	Punctuation: The Toolbelt of Writing	120
	Commas: The "Breath" Marks	121
122	**Test 1: The Foundation Builder**	
	Answer Key and Analysis	156
167	**The "Ready for Game Day" Practice Session**	
	Answer Key	201
213	**Trades Supplemental Practice Vault (Practice 3)**	
214	**The Essential Toolkit: Identification & Use**	
217	**The Hidden Hurdles** **Reasons Good Students Fail (And How You Won't)**	
220	**The Finish Line (and Your New Start)**	
222	**Digital Toolbox**	

Site Prep & Setup - Getting Started

Getting Started: Your Path to the Trades
Congratulations! By deciding to take the Canadian Trades Entrance Exam (TEE), you've already done the hardest part—you've decided to build a better future for yourself. Whether you're looking to get into electrical, plumbing, or any of the great Canadian trades, this exam is the gateway.

I'll be honest with you: there's no sense in sitting for this test unless you're planning to give it your best shot. A high score doesn't just get you in; it shows you've got the grit to handle the work. That means getting organized and learning the right way to tackle the material. It's going to take some real work and a few late nights, but if you put in the time now, that acceptance letter will be sitting in your mailbox before you know it.

We know starting something new can feel a bit like staring at a massive blueprint for the first time—you aren't quite sure where to begin. That's why we're here. We've spent years in the classroom and at the desk, triple-checking our questions to make sure they match what you'll actually see on test day. This guide isn't about fancy theories; it's about giving you the practical tools, "tricks of the trade," and the confidence to walk into that exam room and nail it.

What's on the TEE?
The exam is broken down into three main areas that every tradesperson needs to master:

> **Mathematics:** The numbers you'll use on the job every day.
>
> **Science:** Understanding the physical world and how things actually work.
>
> **Reading Comprehension:** Making sense of the manuals, codes, and specs you'll encounter on a site.
>
> **English:** Grammar and Vocabulary - A separate section here - usually included in the reading section.

A Quick Word of Advice:
While we work hard to keep this guide as up-to-date as a fresh box of tools, exams can change. Sometimes a province adds a new section or tweaks the old ones. Always take a few minutes to carefully read the specific registration materials you get from your local testing centre. It's the first test of your "reading comprehension" skills!

How this study guide is organized

This study guide is divided into four sections. The first section, self-assessments, which will help you recognize your areas of strength and weaknesses. This will be a boon when it comes to managing your study time most efficiently; there is not much point of focusing on material you have already got firmly under control. Instead, taking the self-assessments will show you where that time could be much better spent. In this area you will begin with a few questions to evaluate quickly your understanding of material that is likely to appear on the TEE. If you do poorly in certain areas, simply work carefully through those sections in the tutorials and then try the self-assessment again.

The second section, tutorials, offers information in each of the content areas, as well as strategies to help you master that material. The tutorials are not intended to be a complete course, but cover general principles. If you find that you do not understand the tutorials, it is recommended that you seek out additional instruction.

Third, we offer two sets of practice test questions, similar to those on the TEE Exam.

Your 21-Day "Get-In-The-Trade" Game Plan

This plan assumes you're putting in about 60 to 90 minutes a night. We'll spend the first two weeks building your muscles and the final week sharpening your tools for the big day.

Week 1: The Foundation (Math & Measurement)

In the trades, if your math is off, the whole project is a scrap pile. We start here.

- **Days 1–2: The Basics.** Brush up on whole numbers, decimals, and those tricky fractions. Practice converting a fraction (like 5/8") into a decimal (0.625") until you can do it in your sleep.
- **Days 3–4: Percentages & Ratios.** You'll need these for mixing concrete, calculating slopes, or figuring out tax on a work order.
- **Day 5: Geometry & Measurement.** Dust off the Pythagorean theorem ($a^2 + b^2 = c^2$). You'll use it every time you need to square up a frame or a foundation.
- **Day 6: Basic Algebra.** Practice finding the missing number (x) in simple formulas. It's not "school math"—it's "how much wire do I need" math.
- **Day 7: Rest & Review.** Take 20 minutes to look over the stuff that gave you a headache this week. Then, put the books away.

Week 2: The Moving Parts (Science & Mechanical)

Now we look at how the world actually works on a job site.

- **Days 8–9: Simple Machines.** Study the "Big Six": levers, pulleys, wheels/axles, inclined planes, wedges, and screws. Know how they make work easier (Mechanical Advantage).
- **Days 10–11: Fluids & Heat.** Learn the basics of how water pressure works in a pipe and how metal expands or contracts when the temperature changes.
- **Day 12: Electricity Basics.** You don't need to be an engineer, but you should understand Volts, Amps, and Ohms, and how a basic circuit is completed.
- **Days 13–14: Mechanical Reasoning.** This is the "Spatial Reflex." Practice looking at 2D drawings of gears and belts. If Gear A turns clockwise, which way does Gear Z turn?

Week 3: The Final Polish (Reading & Strategy)

Time to tie it all together and get your "test legs" under you.

- **Days 15–16: Reading for the Trades.** Forget "literature." Practice reading safety manuals, building codes, and work orders. Look for those "Common Traps" like the difference between *mandatory* and *suggested*.
- **Day 17: Vocabulary Check.** Review those workplace words we talked about—words like *intermittent*, *adjacent*, and *precaution*.
- **Days 18–19: Full-Length Practice.** Sit down and do a 50-question practice set. Time yourself. If the real test is 3 hours, try to finish your practice in 2.5.
- **Day 20: The "Weak Link" Fix.** What's still tripping you up? Is it long division? Is it pulleys? Spend tonight fixing that one specific "weak link" in your chain.
- **Day 21: Night Before Prep.** No heavy lifting tonight. Check your ID, make sure you know where the testing centre is, and get to bed early. You've done the work.

Brian's Pro-Tip: Don't try to pull an all-nighter on Day 20. In the trades, a tired worker is a dangerous worker. On a test, a tired brain is a forgetful brain. Trust the process!

MASTERING MATH

This chapter is designed to get your hands dirty with the numbers you'll actually use on the job. Inside, you'll find a Self-Assessment followed by several Math Tutorials.

A quick heads-up: these tutorials aren't a four-year high school curriculum. We've focused on the core principles you need for the trades. We assume you've seen a fraction or a decimal before, but if things feel a bit rusty, don't sweat it. If a section feels like "Greek" to you, that's just a sign to slow down, spend more time on that tutorial, or maybe grab a textbook from the local library for extra reps.

The Mathematics Self-Assessment

Think of this assessment like a diagnostic test on a truck. Its job is to:

Spot the leaks: Identify exactly which areas (like ratios or geometry) need work.

Build your roadmap: Help you decide where to spend your study time.

Get you "Test-Ready": Get you used to the pace and feel of the TEE.

Extra Reps: This assessment is essentially a bonus practice test!

The questions below aren't the exact ones you'll see on the TEE—nobody has a crystal ball, and the exam changes every year. However, they cover the same ground. If you can handle these, you can handle the TEE.

Scoring Your Diagnostic

Once you've finished the assessment, check your score to see where you stand. Here's how to read the results:

Score	Ranking	What it means for you
75% – 100%	Top Notch	You've mastered this stuff. Keep it fresh, but focus your study time elsewhere.
50% – 74%	Fair	You have a working knowledge, but "just passing" can be risky in a competitive trade. Hit the tutorials to shore up your weak spots.
25% – 49%	Needs Work	You're struggling with the core concepts. Take your time with the tutorials, do the practice problems twice, and retake this quiz in a few days.
Under 25%	Back to Basics	You've got some significant gaps. Don't get discouraged—just start from the beginning of the tutorials and work through them slowly before moving to the practice tests.

Mathematics Self-Assessment

	A	B	C	D	E			A	B	C	D	E
1	○	○	○	○	○		21	○	○	○	○	○
2	○	○	○	○	○		22	○	○	○	○	○
3	○	○	○	○	○		23	○	○	○	○	○
4	○	○	○	○	○		24	○	○	○	○	○
5	○	○	○	○	○		25	○	○	○	○	○
6	○	○	○	○	○							
7	○	○	○	○	○							
8	○	○	○	○	○							
9	○	○	○	○	○							
10	○	○	○	○	○							
11	○	○	○	○	○							
12	○	○	○	○	○							
13	○	○	○	○	○							
14	○	○	○	○	○							
15	○	○	○	○	○							
16	○	○	○	○	○							
17	○	○	○	○	○							
18	○	○	○	○	○							
19	○	○	○	○	○							
20	○	○	○	○	○							

1. A plumber has three lengths of copper pipe measuring 1.2 metres, 2.5 metres, and 0.8 metres. What is the total length of pipe?

    a. 3.5 metres
    b. 4.0 metres
    c. 4.5 metres
    d. 5.5 metres

2. An apprentice is cutting pieces of 2x4 lumber. If they start with a 12-foot board and need to cut four pieces that are each 2 feet 3 inches long, how much lumber is left over? (Ignore saw kerf/waste).

    a. 3 feet 0 inches
    b. 4 feet 0 inches
    c. 2 feet 9 inches
    d. 3 feet 6 inches

3. A construction crew needs to pour a concrete pad that requires 15 cubic yards of concrete. If the supplier adds a 10% "waste factor" to the order to ensure they don't run short, how many cubic yards will be delivered?

    a. 1.5 cubic yards
    b. 16.0 cubic yards
    c. 16.5 cubic yards
    d. 17.5 cubic yards

4. What is the decimal equivalent of the fraction 5/8?

    a. 0.58
    b. 0.625
    c. 0.75
    d. 0.85

5. A painter mixes a custom colour using a ratio of 3 parts white paint to 2 parts blue paint. If they use 12 litres of white paint, how many litres of blue paint are required?

    a. 6 litres
    b. 8 litres
    c. 9 litres
    d. 18 litres

6. An electrician is calculating the total load on a circuit. They use the formula: Total = (A + B) × C. If A = 12, B = 8, and C = 1.25, what is the total?

    a. 22
    b. 25
    c. 28
    d. 30

7. A floor is being tiled in a room that measures 4 metres by 5 metres. If the tiles cost $22.50 per square metre, what is the total cost of the tiles?

    a. $450.00
    b. $550.00
    c. $400.00
    d. $422.50

8. Solve the following using BEDMAS: 10 + 5 × 2 - 4

    a. 26
    b. 11
    c. 16
    d. 22

9. A mechanic notes that a bolt requires a 19mm wrench. If they only have imperial wrenches available, which size is the closest equivalent? (1 inch = 25.4 mm).

    a. 1/2 inch
    b. 5/8 inch
    c. 3/4 inch
    d. 7/8 inch

10. A cylindrical water tank has a radius of 1 metre and a height of 3 metres. Using the formula Volume = $\pi \times r^2 \times h$ (where π is approx 3.14), what is the volume of the tank?

    a. 6.28 cubic metres
    b. 9.42 cubic metres
    c. 12.56 cubic metres
    d. 28.26 cubic metres

11. 15 is what percent of 200?

    a. 7.5%
    b. 15%
    c. 20%
    d. 17.50%

12. A boy has 5 red balls, 3 white balls and 2 yellow balls. What percent of the balls are yellow?

    a. 2%
    b. 8%
    c. 20%
    d. 12%

13. Add 10% of 300 to 50% of 20

    a. 50%
    b. 40%
    c. 60%
    d. 45%

14. **Convert 75% to a fraction.**

    a. 2/100
    b. 75/100
    c. 3/4
    d. 4/7

15. **Convert 90% to a fraction**

    a. 1/10
    b. 9/9
    c. 10/100
    d. 9/10

16. **Multiply 3 by 25% of 40**

    a. 75
    b. 30
    c. 68
    d. 35

17. **What is 10% of 30 multiplied by 75% of 200?**

    a. 450
    b. 750
    c. 20
    d. 45

18. **Convert 0.28 to a fraction.**

    a. 7/25
    b. 3.25
    c. 8/25
    d. 5/28

19. Convert 0.45 to a fraction

    a. 7/20
    b. 7/45
    c. 9/20
    d. 3/20

20. Convert 1/5 to percent.

    a. 10%
    b. 5%
    c. 20%
    d. 25%

21. Convert 4/20 to percent

    a. 25%
    b. 20%
    c. 40%
    d. 30%

22. Convert 0.55 to percent

    a. 45%
    b. 15%
    c. 75%
    d. 55%

23. Convert 0.33 to percent

    a. 77%
    b. 67%
    c. 33%
    d. 57%

24. A man buys an item for $420 and has a balance of $3000.00. How much did he have before?

    a. $2,580
    b. $3,420
    c. $2,420
    d. $342

25. Divide 9.60 by 3.2

    a. 2.50
    b. 3
    c. 2.3
    d. 6.4

Answer Key

1. C
1.2 + 2.5 + 0.8 = 4.5

2. A
4 pieces × 2.25 ft = 9 ft. 12 - 9 = 3 ft

3. C
15 × 1.10 = 16.5
Common Trap: Option b is the original amount plus 1, forgetting the percentage calculation.

4. B
5 ÷ 8 = 0.625

5. B
12 / 3 = 4. 4 × 2 = 8

6. B
20 × 1.25 = 25

7. A
20 sq m × 22.50 = 450

8. C
10 + 10 - 4 = 16

9. C
3/4" is approx 19.05mm

10. B
3.14 × 1 × 3 = 9.42

11. A
15% = 15/100 X 200 = 7.5%

12. C
Total no. of balls = 10, no. of yellow balls = 2. 2/10 X 100 = 20%

13. B
10% of 300 = 30 and 50% of 20 = 10 so 30 + 10 = 40.

14. C
75%= 75/100 = ¾

15. D
90% = 90/100 = 9/10

16. B
25% of 40 = 10 and 10 x 3 = 30

17. A
10% of 30 = 3 and 75% of 200 = 150, 3 X 150 = 450

18. A
0.28 = 28/100 = 7/25

19. C
0.45 = 45/100 = 9/20

20. C
1/5 X 100 = 20%

21. B
4/20 X 100 = 1/5 X 100 = 20%

22. D
0.55 X 100 = 55%

23. C
0.33 X 100 = 33%

24. B
(Amount Spent) $420 + $3000 (Balance) = $3420

25. B
9.60/3.2 = 3

Basic Math Video Tutorials

https://www.test-preparation.ca/math-videos/

How to Answer Basic Math Multiple Choice

The time allowed on the math portion of a standardized test is typically so short that there's no room for error. You have to be fast and accurate.

Math strategy is very helpful, but nothing beats knowing your stuff! Make sure that you have learned all the important formulas that will be used.

If you don't know the formulas, strategy won't help you.

How to Answer Basic Math Questions - the Basics

First, read the problem, but not the answers.

Work through the problem first and come up with your own answers. Hopefully, you should find your answer among the choices.

If no answer matches the one you got, re-check your math, but this time, use a different method. In math, there are different ways to solve a problem.

Math Multiple Choice Strategy

The two strategies for working with basic math multiple choice are Estimation and Elimination.

Estimation is just as it sounds - try to estimate an approximate answer first. Then look at the choices.

Elimination is probably the most powerful strategy for answering multiple choice.
Eliminate obviously incorrect answers and narrowing the possible choices.

Here are a few basic math examples of how this works.

Solve 2/3 + 5/12

    a. 9/17

    b. 3/11

    c. 7/12

    d. 1 1/12

First estimate the answer. 2/3 is more than half and 5/12 is about half, so the answer is going to be very close to 1.

Next, Eliminate. Choice A is about 1/2 and can be eliminated, choice B is very small, less than 1/2 and can be eliminated. Choice C is close to 1/2 and can be eliminated. Leaving only choice D, which is just over 1.

Work through the solution, find a common denominator and add. The correct answer is 1 1/12, so Choice D is correct.

Let's look at another example:

Solve 4/5 – 2/3

    a. 2/2
    b. 2/13
    c. 1
    d. 2/15

First, quickly estimate the answer. 4/5 is very close to 1, and 2/3 more than half, so the answer is going to be less than 1/2.

Choice A can be eliminated right away, because it is 1. Choice C can be eliminated for the same reason.

Next, look at the denominators. Since 5 and 3 don't go into 13, choice B can be eliminated as well.

That leaves choice D. Checking the answer, the common denominator will be 15. So the answer is 2/15 and choice D is correct.

Order Of Operation

Some math calculations contain more than one set of operations. For example, a problem like 3 + (35 - 21) x 2 requires addition, subtraction and multiplication operations. The problem arises from the confusion of which of the operations to perform first. Starting with the wrong operation will give you the wrong answer. To solve this dilemma and to avoid confusion, the Order of Operation rules were set.

Order of operation is a set of mathematical rules designed to be used for calculations that require more than one arithmetic operation. For example, calculation problems that require two or more out of addition, subtraction, multiplication and division, would require that you follow the order of operation to solve.

The order of operation rules are quite simple as explained below.

> **Rule 1:** Start with calculations that are inside brackets or parentheses.
> **Rule 2:** Then, solve all multiplications and divisions, from left to right.
> **Rule 3:** Finally, solve all additions and subtractions, from left to right.

Example 1

Solve 16 + 5 x 8

Based on the rules above, we would have to start with the multiplication part of the question.
That will give: 16 + 40 = 56

Take note that if the rule was not followed and addition was done first, the answer gotten would be different and wrong.

16 + 5 x 8
21 x 8 = 168 (wrong answer)

Example 2

3 +(35 - 21) x 2

Based on the rules of the order of operation, we have to solve the problem in the bracket or parenthesis first. Then we do the multiplication, before doing the addition.

3 + (35 - 21) x 2

3 + (14) x 2
3 + 28
= 31

Decimal Tips, Tricks and Shortcuts

CONVERTING DECIMALS TO FRACTIONS

Converting decimals to fractions is easy if you say it the right way! If you say "point one" or "point 25," you'll have trouble.

But if you say, "one tenth" and "twenty-five hundredths," then you have already solved it! That's because, if you know your fractions, you know that "one tenth" looks like this: 1/10. And "twenty-five hundredths" looks like this: 25/100.

Even if you have digits before the decimal, such as 3.4, learning how to say the word will help you with the conversion into a fraction. It's not "three point four," it's "three and four tenths." Knowing this, you know that the fraction which looks like "three and four tenths" is 3 4/10.

The conversion is not complete until you reduce the fraction to its lowest terms: It's not 25/100, but 1/4.

Converting Decimals to Percent

Changing a decimal to a percent is easy if you remember one thing: multiply by 100.

For example, if you start with .45, simply multiply it by 100 for 45. Then add the % sign to the end - 45%.

Think of it this way: take out the decimal point, add a percent sign on the opposite side. In other words, the decimal on the left is replaced by the % on the right.

It doesn't work quite that easily if the decimal is in the middle of the number. For example, 3.7. Here, take out the decimal in the middle and replace it with a 0 % at the end. So 3.7 converted to decimal is 370%.

Percent Tips, Tricks and Short-cuts

Percent problems are not nearly as scary as they appear, if you remember this neat trick:

Draw a cross as in:

Portion	Percent
Whole	100

In the upper left, write PORTION. In the bottom left write WHOLE. In the top right, write PERCENT and in the bottom right, write 100. Whatever your problem is, you will leave blank the unknown, and fill in the other four parts. For example, let's suppose your problem is: Find 10% of 50. Since we know the 10% part, we put 10 in the percent corner. Since the whole number in our problem is 50, we put that in the corner marked whole. You always put 100 underneath the percent, so we leave it as is, which leaves only the top left corner blank. This is where we'll put our answer. Now simply multiply the two corner numbers that are NOT 100. Here, it's 10 X 50. That gives us 500. Now divide this by the remaining corner, or 100, to get a final answer of 5. 5 is the number that goes in the upper-left corner, and is your final solution.

Another hint to remember: Percents are the same thing as hundredths in decimals. So .45 is the same as 45 hundredths or 45 percent.

Percent Tips and Tricks Video

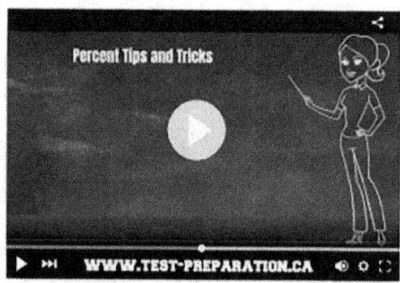

https://youtu.be/T9qiEHzwJEU?si=Vvo_WY8sdTPhF8S7

Converting Percents to Decimals

Percents are just a type of decimal, so it should be no surprise that converting between the two is actually fairly simple. Here are a few tricks and Short-cuts to keep in mind:

- Remember that percent literally means "per 100" or "for every 100." So when you speak of 30% you're saying 30 for every 100 or the fraction 30/100. In

basic math, you learned that fractions that have 10 or 100 as the denominator can easily be turned to a decimal. 30/100 is thirty hundredths, or expressed as a decimal, .30.
- ☐ Another way to look at it: To convert a percent to a decimal, simply divide the number by 100. So for instance, if the percent is 47%, divide 47 by 100. The result will be .47. Get rid of the % mark and you're done.

- ☐ Remember that the easiest way of dividing by 100 is by moving your decimal two spots to the left.

Converting Percents to Fractions

Converting percents to fractions is easy. After all, a percent is just a type of fraction; it tells you what part of 100 that you're talking about. Here are some simple ideas for making the conversion from a percent to a fraction:

- ☐ If the percent is a whole number -- say 34% -- then simply write a fraction with 100 as the denominator (the bottom number). Then put the percentage itself on top. So 34% becomes 34/100.
- ☐ Now reduce as you would reduce any percent. Here, by dividing 2 into 34 and 2 into 100, you get 17/50.
- ☐ If your percent is not a whole number -- say 3.4% --then convert it to a decimal expressed as hundredths. 3.4 is the same as 3.40 (or 3 and forty hundredths). Now ask yourself how you would express "three and forty hundredths" as a fraction. It would, of course, be 3 40/100. Reduce this and it becomes 3 2/5.

Fraction Tips, Tricks and Short-cuts

When you are writing an exam, time is precious, so anything you can do to answer questions faster is a real advantage.

Here are some ideas, Short-cuts, tips and tricks that can

speed up answering fraction problems.

Remember that a fraction is just a number which names a portion of something. For instance, instead of having a whole pie, a fraction says you have a part of a pie--such as a half of one or a fourth of one.

Two numbers make up a fraction. The number on top is the numerator. The number on the bottom is the denominator.

To remember which is which, just remember that "denominator" and "down" both start with a "d." And the "downstairs" number is the denominator. So for instance, in ½, the numerator is 1, and the denominator (or "downstairs") number is 2.

Adding Fractions

It's easy to add two fractions if they have the same denominator. Just add the digits on top and leave the bottom one the same: 1/10 + 6/10 = 7/10.

It's the same with subtracting fractions with the same denominator: 7/10 - 6/10 = 1/10.

Adding and subtracting fractions with different denominators is a little more complicated.

First, you have to arrange the fractions so they have the same denominators.

The easiest way to do this is to multiply the denominators: For 2/5 + 1/2 multiply 5 by 2. Now you have a denominator of 10.

But now you have to change the top numbers too. Since you multiplied the 5 in 2/5 by 2, you also multiply the 2 by 2, to get 4. So the first fraction is now 4/10.

In the second fraction, you multiplied the denominator by 5, you have to multiply the numerator by 5 also, to get 5/10.

Now you have 4/10 + 5/10 and you can add 5 and 4 to get 9/10.

Simplest Form

To reduce a fraction to its simplest form, you have to arrange the numerator and denominator so the only common factor is 1.

Think of it this way:

Let's take an example: The fraction 2/10.

This is not reduced to its simplest terms because there is a number that will divide evenly into both: 2. We want to make it so that the only number that will divide evenly into both is 1.

Divide the top and bottom by 2 to get the new, reduced fraction - 1/5.

Multiplying Fractions

This is the easiest of all: Just multiply the two top numbers and then multiply the two bottom numbers.

Here is an example,

2/5 X 2/3

First, multiply the numerators: 2 X 2 = 4

then multiply the denominators: 5 X 3 = 15

Your answer is 4/15.

Dividing Fractions

Dividing fractions is easy if you remember a simple trick - first turn the second fraction upside down - then multiply!

Here is an example:

7/8 X 1/2

Turn the second fraction upside down:

7/8 X 2/1

then multiply:

(7 X 2) / (8 X 1) = 14/8

Converting Fractions to Decimals

There are a couple of ways to convert fractions to decimals. The first, which is the fastest -- is to memorize some basic fraction facts.

1/100 is "one hundredth," expressed as a decimal, it's .01.

1/50 is "two hundredths," expressed as a decimal, it's .02.

1/25 is "one twenty-fifth" or "four hundredths," expressed as a decimal, it's .04.

1/20 is "one twentieth" or ""five hundredths," expressed as a decimal, it's .05.

1/10 is "one tenth," expressed as a decimal, it's .1.

1/8 is "one eighth," or "one hundred twenty-five thousandths," expressed as a decimal, it's .125.

1/5 is "one fifth," or "two tenths," expressed as a decimal, it's .2.

1/4 is "one fourth" or "twenty-five hundredths," expressed as a decimal, it's .25.

1/3 is "one third" or "thirty-three hundredths," expressed as a decimal, it's .33.

1/2 is "one half" or "five tenths," expressed as a decimal, it's .5.

3/4 is "three fourths," or "seventy-five hundredths," expressed as a decimal, it's .75.

Of course, if you're no good at memorization, another good technique for converting a fraction to a decimal is to manipulate it so that the fraction's denominator is 10, 100, 1000, or some other power of 10.

Here's an example: We'll start with three quarters. What is the first number in the 4 "times table" that you can multiply and get a multiple of 10? Can you multiply 4 by something to get 10? No. Can you multiply it by something to get 100? Yes! 4 X 25 is 100.

So multiply the numerator by 25, which is 75 over 100

We know fractions are really a division problem, and we also know that dividing by 100, means we move the decimal 2 places to the left.

So, 75 over 100 = .75

Lets try another example - Convert one fifth to a decimal.

First find a power of 10 that 5 goes into evenly, which is 2.

Multiply the numerator and denominator by 2, which is

two tenths.

Dividing 2 by 10 means we move the decimal place 1 place to the left.

So 1/5 = 0.5

Converting Fractions to Percent

Here is a quick method to convert fraction to percent and a strategy for answering on a multiple choice test that will save you valuable exam time.

First, remember that a fraction is a division problem: you're dividing the bottom number into the top.

Taking an example, convert 2/3 into percent.

The first method is to multiple the numerator by 100 and

divide. So,

(2 X 100) / 2 = 100/3 = 66.66

Add a % sign and you have the answer, 66.66%

https://youtu.be/T9qiEHzwJEU?si=ZF9qVNLEF6JnPgqm

If you're doing these conversions on a multiple-choice test, here's an idea that might be even easier and faster. Let's say you have a fraction of 1/8 and you're asked to convert to percent.

Since we know that "percent" means hundredths, ask yourself what number we can multiply 8 by to get 100. Since there is no number, ask what number gets us close to 100.

That number is 12: 8 X 12 = 96. So it gets us a little less than 100. Now, whatever you do to the denominator, you have to do to the numerator. Let's multiply 1 X 12 and we get 12. However, since 96 is a little less than 100, we know that our answer will be a little MORE than 12%.

Look at the choices and eliminate the obvious wrong choices. So if your possible answers on the multiple-choice test are these:

a) 8.5% b) 19% c) 12.5% d) 25%

then we know the answer is c) 12.5%, because it's a little MORE than the 12 we got in our math problem above.

Here all the choices except choice C 12.5% can be eliminated.

You don't have to know the exact correct answer, just enough to estimate, then eliminate the obviously wrong answers.

This was an easy example to demonstrate the strategy, but don't be fooled! You probably won't get such an easy question on your exam. By estimating your answer quickly, then eliminating obviously incorrect choices immediately, you save precious exam time.

Most Common Fraction Mistakes on a Test

1. Not simplifying fractions first. Always simplify fractions to the simples form before adding, subtracting or other operations.

2. Not understanding common denominators.

To add or subtract fractions, they must have the same denominator. For example, to add 1/2 and 3/4, a common denominator is needed. The common denominator 4, because 4 is a multiple of both 2 and 4.

So, you would convert 1/2 to 2/4 and add it to 3/4 to get 2/4 + 3/4 = 5/4

3. Errors with mixed numbers and converting to improper fractions or vice versa.

Referring to the problem above, 5/4 is an improper fraction, since 5 (the numerator) is larger than 4 (the denominator). This can be converted to a mixed number – 5/4 = 4/4 + 1/4, and we know 4/4 = 1

so – 1 + 1/4 = 1 1/4.

4. Errors with equivalent fractions and reducing to the simplest form.

Here is question – Does 2/4 = 1/2 ? YES! we can reduce 2/4 by dividing the numerator (top) and the denominator (bottom) by 2. so 2/4 divided by 2/2 = 1/2.

5. Errors canceling common factors in fractions.

Cancelling out common factors works like this – 2/4 X 4/8 These are divisible by 2 so we divide by 2 in the top of one side and bottom of the other – 1/4 X 4/4

We can do the same again with the bottom of the first fraction and the top of the second – 1/1 X 1/4 and since 1/1 = 1 we have 1 X 1/4 = 1/4.

6. Errors with basic arithmetic operations (addition, subtraction, multiplication, and division) with fractions.

TRADES SCIENCE
HOW THINGS
WORK

Science for the Real World

Welcome to the Science section. In the trades, "science" isn't just something that happens in a lab with a white coat; it's what happens when metal expands in the heat, how a pulley lifts a heavy load, or why certain chemicals shouldn't be mixed in a bucket.

This chapter includes a Science Self-Assessment and a series of Tutorials. We've designed these to refresh your memory on the general principles you'll face on the TEE. Now, we'll be straight with you: these tutorials aren't a substitute for a full semester of high school or university science. We assume you've got a basic handle on the natural world, but if a section feels like a different language, that's your cue to seek out some extra resources or spend a few extra nights on that specific tutorial.

What's Under the Hood? (TEE Science Topics)

Here's a quick tour of the territory we'll be covering. These are the "big hitters" that show up most often on the exam:

Simple Machines: Levers, pulleys, gears, and inclined planes. Students need to understand mechanical advantage without needing a lab coat.

Properties of Matter: Basic chemistry (WHMIS labels, flashpoints, and reactivity) and physical states (solids, liquids, gases).

Energy & Heat: Temperature conversion (Celsius to Fahrenheit), heat transfer (conduction/convection), and basic pressure (hydraulics and pneumatics).

Electricity Basics: Understanding the relationship between Volts, Amps, and Ohms.

Your Science Self-Assessment

Think of this as a "pre-trip inspection." You wouldn't drive a rig across the Coquihalla without checking the brakes, and you shouldn't dive into your final prep without knowing where your knowledge stands.

The questions in this assessment cover the same ground as the TEE, but they aren't the exact questions you'll see on test day. The test-makers love to swap questions, change the timing, or tweak the format from year to year. Our goal is to make sure you understand the principles. If you understand the "why," the "how" of the question won't trip you up.

Why take this assessment?

To find your "leaks" (strengths and weaknesses).

To help you build your 3-week study plan (see Chapter 1).

To get your brain used to the TEE's "vibe."

To get some extra practice reps under your belt.

Gauging Your Results

Since this is a self-assessment, don't worry about the clock too much yet—just focus on accuracy. Once you're done, use the table below to see where you need to put in the work.

The goal here is to give you a baseline score. Once you finish, look at the table below to see how you stack up and what your next move should be.

Scoring Guide: Where Do You Stand?

Score Range	What it Means	Your Next Step
80% - 100%	You've got a sharp eye for detail.	Focus on your weaker subjects; just do a light review here.
60% - 79%	You're on the right track, but missing the finer points.	Go through the tutorials again and practice active reading.
Below 60%	This area is going to be a struggle on exam day.	Dig deep into the tutorials and consider extra reading exercises.

Science Self Assessment

	A	B	C	D	E			A	B	C	D	E
1	○	○	○	○	○		21	○	○	○	○	○
2	○	○	○	○	○		22	○	○	○	○	○
3	○	○	○	○	○		23	○	○	○	○	○
4	○	○	○	○	○		24	○	○	○	○	○
5	○	○	○	○	○		25	○	○	○	○	○
6	○	○	○	○	○		26	○	○	○	○	○
7	○	○	○	○	○		27	○	○	○	○	○
8	○	○	○	○	○		28	○	○	○	○	○
9	○	○	○	○	○		29	○	○	○	○	○
10	○	○	○	○	○		30	○	○	○	○	○
11	○	○	○	○	○							
12	○	○	○	○	○							
13	○	○	○	○	○							
14	○	○	○	○	○							
15	○	○	○	○	○							
16	○	○	○	○	○							
17	○	○	○	○	○							
18	○	○	○	○	○							
19	○	○	○	○	○							
20	○	○	○	○	○							

1. Which simple machine consists of a rigid bar that pivots on a fixed point called a fulcrum?

   a. Pulley

   b. Lever

   c. Inclined plane

   d. Gear

2. An apprentice is using a crowbar to lift a heavy crate. If the apprentice moves the fulcrum closer to the crate, what happens to the effort required to lift it?

   a. The effort increases because the resistance arm is longer.

   b. The effort decreases because the mechanical advantage increases.

   c. The effort stays the same but the distance moved increases.

   d. The effort increases because the effort arm is now shorter.

3. You are using a ramp (inclined plane) to load a 200 kg generator onto a truck bed. If you replace the current ramp with one that is twice as long but reaches the same height, how does the required force change?

   a. The force required is doubled.

   b. The force required is cut in half.

   c. The force remains the same, but you do twice the work.

   d. The force required increases due to increased friction over distance.

4. A technician is inspecting a gear assembly where a small drive gear is turning a much larger driven gear. The technician notes that the machine has high torque but moves very slowly. If the goal is to increase the speed of the output shaft while sacrificing torque, what change should be made?

    a. Increase the number of teeth on the driven gear.

    b. Decrease the number of teeth on the drive gear.

    c. Use a drive gear and driven gear of equal size.

    d. Increase the number of teeth on the drive gear.

5. In the WHMIS system, which symbol is used to identify materials that can cause immediate and severe health effects or death after even short-term exposure?

    a. Flame

    b. Skull and Crossbones

    c. Exclamation Mark

    d. Health Hazard (person with star)

6. A worker is handling a cleaning solvent and notices the label indicates a very low "flashpoint." What is the most important safety precaution to take based on this information?

    a. Wear a heavy rubber apron to prevent skin absorption.

    b. Keep the container away from any spark or open flame.

    c. Ensure the room is kept at freezing temperatures.

    d. Use the solvent only in high-pressure environments.

7. While working in a shop in BC, you find a container where the liquid inside has a pH of 2. How should this substance be categorized and handled?

    a. It is a strong base and should be neutralized with vinegar.

    b. It is a neutral substance like water and requires no special gear.

    c. It is a strong acid and is likely corrosive to skin and metal.

    d. It is a compressed gas that has liquified under pressure.

8. Which of the following describes the transition of a substance directly from a solid state to a gaseous state without becoming a liquid first?

    a. Evaporation

    b. Condensation

    c. Sublimation

    d. Melting

9. You are monitoring a hydraulic press. You notice that even though the pump is running, the piston is moving jerkily and making a "spongy" sound. What is the most likely scientific cause of this mechanical failure?

    a. The hydraulic fluid has become a solid due to cold.

    b. Air has entered the system and is compressing, unlike the fluid.

    c. The fluid is too dense to pass through the valves.

    d. The pressure has caused the metal casing to expand.

10. A thermometer in the shop reads 25 degrees Celsius. A visitor from the US asks what that is in Fahrenheit. Using the formula F = (C · 1.8) + 32, what is the temperature?

    a. 45 F

    b. 77 F

    c. 82 F

    d. 65 F

11. A metal rod is placed with one end in a furnace and the other end held by a worker wearing a glove. Over time, the end held by the worker becomes hot. Which method of heat transfer is primarily responsible for this?

    a. Convection

    b. Radiation

    c. Conduction

    d. Induction

12. Which electrical unit measures the "pressure" or force that pushes electrons through a circuit?

    a. Amps

    b. Ohms

    c. Watts

    d. Volts

13. A circuit has a resistance of 10 Ohms and a voltage of 120 Volts. According to Ohm's Law ($V = I \times R$), what is the current (Amperage) flowing through the circuit?

    a. 1,200 Amps

    b. 12 Amps

    c. 130 Amps

    d. 0.08 Amps

14. A portable heater is plugged into a long, thin extension cord. The heater isn't getting as hot as it should, and the cord is feeling warm. Scientifically, why is the heater's performance reduced?

    a. The cord is creating too much Voltage for the heater to handle.

    b. The thin cord has high resistance, causing a voltage drop before it reaches the heater.

    c. The heater is drawing more Amps than the wall outlet can provide.

    d. The cord is acting as an insulator, trapping the electricity inside.

15. What happens to the molecules of a gas when the gas is heated in a sealed, rigid container?

    a. They slow down and take up less space.

    b. They move faster and hit the walls with more force, increasing pressure.

    c. They turn into a solid state.

    d. They shrink in size but increase in number.

16. You are using a fixed pulley to lift a heavy bucket of tools to a roof. If the bucket weighs 50 lbs, how much force must you pull with (ignoring friction)?

    a. 25 lbs

    b. 50 lbs

    c. 100 lbs

    d. 10 lbs

17. A worker needs to loosen a rusted bolt. They find that using a standard 10-inch wrench isn't working. Why would switching to a 24-inch "cheater bar" or a longer wrench help?

    a. It increases the RPM of the bolt.

    b. It increases the torque by increasing the distance from the fulcrum.

    c. It changes the direction of the force applied.

    d. It reduces the friction between the bolt and the threads.

18. What is the standard unit of measurement for resistance in an electrical circuit?

    a. Ampere

    b. Ohm

    c. Volt

    d. Joule

19. An HVAC tech is working on a cooling system. They notice that as the refrigerant gas is compressed by the compressor, the temperature of the gas rises significantly. This is an example of:

    a. The Law of Conservation of Mass.

    b. Heat of compression (Gas Law relationship between pressure and temperature).

    c. The cooling effect of evaporation.

    d. Electrical resistance in the compressor motor.

20. You see a WHMIS label with an "Exclamation Mark" in a red diamond. This indicates the product:

    a. Is explosive.

    b. Is a gas under pressure.

    c. May cause less severe health effects like skin irritation or sensitization.

    d. Is flammable and should be kept away from heat.

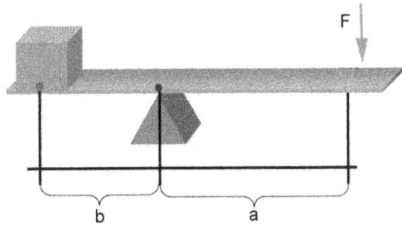

21. Consider the illustration above and the corresponding data:

Weight = W = 200 pounds
Distance from fulcrum to Weight = b = 10 feet
Distance from fulcrum to point where force is applied = a = 20 feet
How much force (F) must be applied to lift the weight?

    a. 80

    b. 100

    c. 150

    d. 200

22. A force of 20 kg. is applied to two springs in series, which compresses the springs 6 inches. If the same force is applied to springs in parallel, how far will the springs compress?

    a. 6 inches

    b. 3 inches

    c. 2 inches

    d. 1 inch

23. You are asked to determine the gear ratio of a vehicle. You open the differential and observe the ring gear the and pinion gear. The ring gear has 40 teeth and the pinion gear has 8, What is the gear ratio of the vehicle?

    a. 4:1
    b. 5:1
    c. 8:2
    d. 8:0

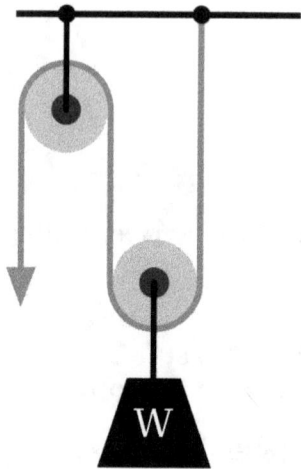

24. Consider the pulley arrangement above. If the weight, W, is 50 pounds, how much force is required to lift it?

    a. 10 pounds
    b. 20 pounds
    c. 25 pounds
    d. 50 pounds

25. Consider a gear train with 3 gears, from left to right, A with 20 teeth, gear B with 60 teeth, and gear C with 10 teeth. Gear A turns clockwise at 60 rpm. What direction and speed in rpm does Gear C turn?

    a. 120 rpm, clockwise

    b. 100 rpm clockwise

    c. 120 rpm counter clockwise

    d. 140 rpm counter clockwise

26. If a 100-pound object is sitting on a 10-square-inch plate, what is the PSI?

    a. 5

    b. 10

    c. 15

    d. 20

27. What is mechanical advantage?

    a. The ratio of energy input to energy output, typically where the input is less than the output.

    b. The ratio of energy input to energy output, typically where the input is greater than the output.

    c. The ratio of energy resistance to energy output, typically where the resistance is less than the output.

    d. None of the above

28. What is the ratio of mechanical advantage of a simple pulley?

    a. 2:1

    b. 1:1

    c. 3:1

    d. 1:2

29. **Consider moving an object with a lever and a fulcrum. What is the relationship between the distance from the fulcrum and the speed the object will move?**

   a. The farther away from the fulcrum, the faster the object will move.

   b. The closer to the fulcrum, the faster an object will move.

   c. An object will move the fastest when directly above the fulcrum.

   d. None of the above.

30. **Which of the following are examples of a wedge?**

   a. Corkscrew

   b. Scissors

   c. Wheelbarrow

   d. Pulley

Answer Key

1. B
A lever uses a fulcrum to pivot.

2. B
Moving the fulcrum closer to the load shortens the resistance arm and lengthens the effort arm, increasing mechanical advantage.

Common Trap: Option d is the trap; if you move it away from the load, the effort arm gets shorter, but the question says closer.

3. B
Doubling the length of the ramp while keeping height the same cuts the slope in half, doubling the mechanical advantage and halving the force required.

4. D
A larger drive gear turns the driven gear faster but with less torque.

5. B
Skull and crossbones indicates acute toxicity.

6. B
A low flashpoint means the liquid ignites at low temperatures.

Common Trap: Option c suggests freezing it; while cold helps, "keep away from sparks" is the standard shop safety protocol.

7. C
A pH of 2 is highly acidic (0-6 is acidic, 7 is neutral, 8-14 is basic).

8. C
Sublimation is the phase change from solid to gas (like dry ice).

9. B
Liquids don't compress, but gases do. Air in a hydraulic line makes it "spongy."

10. B
(25 X 1.8) + 32 = 45 + 32 = 77.

11. C
Conduction is heat transfer through direct contact in solids.

12. D
Voltage is electrical potential/pressure.

13. B
120 / 10 = 12.

14. B
Long/thin wires increase resistance, causing "Voltage Drop."

Common Trap: Option c; a heater draws Amps, but the scientific reason for the cord heat and low performance is the resistance/drop.

15. B
Heat increases kinetic energy in gas molecules.

16. B
A single fixed pulley only changes the direction of force, it doesn't provide mechanical advantage.

17. B
Torque = Force x Distance. More distance = more torque for the same effort.

18. B
Ohms measure resistance.

19. B
Charles's and Boyle's laws explain how pressure, volume, and temperature relate.

20. C
The exclamation mark is for "lesser" hazards like irritation.

21. B
To solve for F, Weight X b (distance from fulcrum to weight) = Force X a (distance from fulcrum to point where force is applied)
200 X 10 = F X 20
2000/20 = F
F = 100

22. B
If the springs in series compress 6 inches, then the springs in parallel will compress half that amount, or 3 inches.

23. B
Opening the differential, the ring gear is the larger gear and the pinion the smaller. The gear differential is calculated by dividing the number of teeth on the pinion into the number of teeth on the ring gear. 40/8 = 5, or 5:1.

24. C
Since the weight is only attached to one pulley, the force required will be 50/2 = 25 pounds.

25. A
First calculate the speed of gear B. The gear ratio is 60:20 or 3:1. If gear A is turning at 60 rpm, then gear B will turn at 30/3 = 20 rpm.

Next calculate B and C. Gear C is smaller, so it will turn faster. The gear ratio is 60:10 or 6:1, and since gear B turns at 20 rpm, gear C will turn at 20 X 6 = 120 rpm.

Next calculate the direction. Gear A is turning clockwise, so Gear B is turning counter-clockwise, so gear C must be turning clockwise.

26. B
Calculate the PSI by taking the weight divided by the size of the object the weight is bearing on. 100/10 = 10 PSI.

27. A
Mechanical advantage is the ratio of energy input to energy output, typically where the input is less than the output. Mechanical advantage is a measure of the force amplification

achieved by using a tool, mechanical device or machine system. Ideally, the device preserves the input power and simply trades off forces against movement to obtain a desired amplification in the output force. The model for this is the law of the lever. Machine components designed to manage forces and movement in this way are called mechanisms.

28. B
The ratio of mechanical advantage of a simple pulley is 1:1.

29. A
The farther away from the fulcrum, the faster the object will move.

30. B
Examples of wedges include the cutting edge of scissors, knives, screwdrivers, doorstops, nails axes and chisels.

Overview of Simple Machines

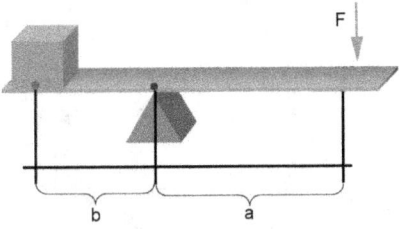

Levers

The Lever: Work Smarter, Not Harder
At its simplest, a lever is just a sturdy bar and a pivot point, which we call the fulcrum. It's the oldest trick in the book for moving something heavy that doesn't want to budge.

The "magic" of a lever comes down to distance. Think of it this way: the further you are from the pivot point, the more "oomph" (torque) you have. If you've ever used a long pipe to get a rusted nut moving, you've already mastered the science of the shop.

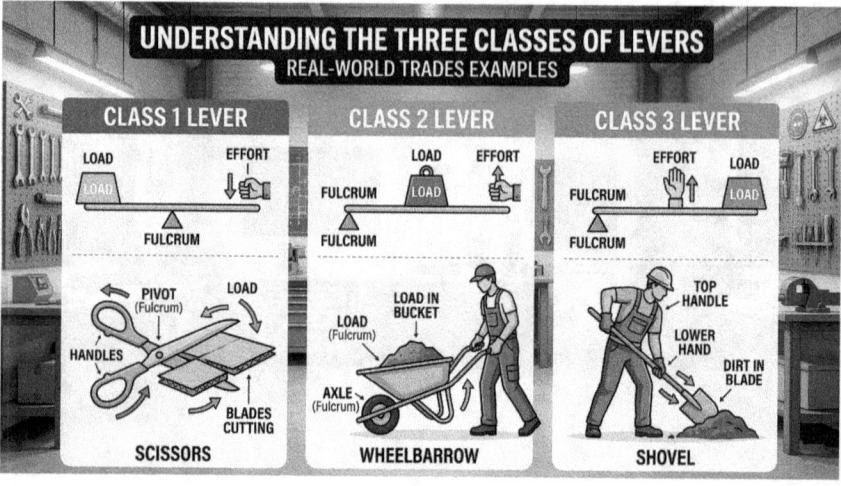

The Golden Rule of Leverage

There is a trade-off in every machine. If the lever makes a heavy weight feel light, you have to move your end of the bar a longer distance to get that weight to move just a little bit.

> **Longer Handle (Input Arm):** Less effort is needed, but you have to push the handle further.

> **Shorter Handle (Input Arm):** More effort is needed, but the weight moves faster.

Brian's Pro Tip: When you're looking at a lever problem, always identify the fulcrum first. Then, measure how far the weight is from it, and how far your hands are from it. That's the key to the whole puzzle.

Let's Put it to Work
Imagine you're using a pry bar to lift a piece of heavy machinery.

The Data:

Weight (W): 100 pounds

Distance from Weight to Pivot (b): 2 feet

Distance from Your Hands to Pivot (a): 5 feet

The Goal: How much force (F) do you actually need to lean on that bar with to get the machine to lift?

The Solution:
In the shop, we use a simple balance equation. The weight multiplied by its distance must be balanced by your force multiplied by your distance.

Weight × b = Force × a
100 lbs × 2 ft = F × 5 ft
200 = F × 5
Now, just divide that 200 by the 5 feet of "reach" you have:

200/5 = 40

Answer: You only need to apply 40 pounds of force to lift that 100-pound weight. That's the "Mechanical Advantage" in action—making you 2.5 times stronger than you'd be without the bar.

Pulleys

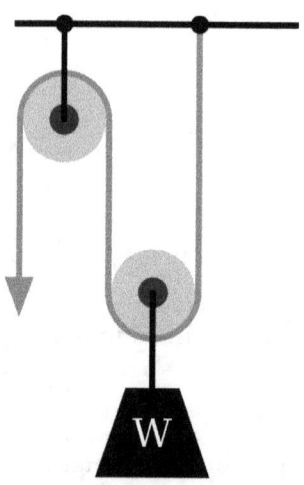

Pulleys: Multiplying Your Strength

A pulley (sometimes called a **sheave** or a **drum**) is essentially a wheel with a groove that holds a rope, cable, or belt. While a single fixed pulley just changes the direction you pull, hooking multiple pulleys together creates a Block and Tackle. This is where the real work gets done.

The "Rope Trick" for Mechanical Advantage
You don't need a physics degree to figure out how much a pulley system will help you. In the shop, we use the **Count the Ropes** rule.

If you have a continuous rope running through a set of pulleys, your **Mechanical Advantage** is simply the number of rope sections actually supporting the weight you are lifting.

> **The Rule:** If you have 4 ropes pulling up on a heavy crate, the crate "feels" 4 times lighter to you.

> **The Trade-off:** Just like with levers, there's no free lunch. If the crate feels 4 times lighter, you have to pull 4 times more rope to lift it the same distance.

Let's Put it to Work
Imagine you are using a block and tackle system to lift a 600-pound engine block out of a truck. You count the ropes attached to the bottom pulley (the one moving the engine) and see there are 3 rope sections supporting the load.

The Data:

Weight (W): 600 pounds

Number of supporting ropes (p): 3

The Goal: How much force (T) do you need to pull with to lift the engine?

The Solution:
To find your input force, you just divide the total weight by the number of supporting ropes.

T = W/p
T = 600 lbs/3
T = 200

Answer: You only need to pull with 200 pounds of force to move that 600-pound engine.

Brian's Pro Tip: When you're looking at a diagram on the test, ignore the part of the rope you are actually holding (the "lead line") if you are pulling down. Only count the ropes that are physically pulling the weight up.

The Wedge: Splitting and Lifting

A wedge is basically just two ramps (inclined planes) joined back-to-back. Instead of moving a load up a ramp, you're driving the ramp into the load. Whether you're splitting a log or shimming a heavy piece of equipment to get it level, you're using a wedge.

How it Works: The Trade-off
The job of a wedge is to take a force coming from one direction (like a hammer strike) and turn it into a much stronger force pushing outward or upward.

> **Long, Thin Wedge:** These have a high Mechanical Advantage. They are easier to drive in, but you have to drive them a long way to get much movement.
>
> **Short, Fat Wedge:** These are harder to drive in (they require more "grunt"), but they move things apart much faster.

Brian's Pro Tip: Think of a wedge like a gear. A long, skinny wedge is like "low gear"—lots of power, but you move slowly. A fat wedge is "high gear"—it moves fast but takes a lot of force to get started.

Let's Put it to Work
Imagine you are a finishing carpenter in Victoria, and you're trying to lift the corner of a heavy cabinet just 1/4 of an inch so you can slide a permanent base under it. You decide to use a wooden shim (a wedge).

The Data:

Length of the wedge (L): 6 inches

Thickness/Width at the fat end (W): 1 inch

The Goal: What is the Mechanical Advantage (MA) of this shim?

The Solution:
To find the advantage of a wedge, you just divide the length by the thickness. It's that simple.

MA = Length/Width
MA = 6 inches/1 inch
MA = 6

Answer: This wedge has a Mechanical Advantage of 6. This means for every 10 pounds of force you use to tap that shim in with your hammer, the wedge is pushing "up" with 60 pounds of force.

The Screw: The Circular Ramp

Think of a screw like a spiral staircase. To get to the top floor, you have to walk a long way around the circle, but it's much easier than trying to climb straight up a ladder.

How it Works: Pitch and Lead
The "magic" of the screw comes down to the Pitch. The pitch is simply the distance between one thread and the next.

> **Fine Threads (Small Pitch):** The threads are close together. This gives you a huge Mechanical Advantage. It's easy to turn, but you have to spin it a lot of times to get it to move forward just an inch.

> **Coarse Threads (Large Pitch):** The threads are further apart. It takes more "grunt" to turn, but it moves into the material much faster.

Brian's Pro Tip: If you're struggling to tighten a bolt, remember that a longer wrench handle (like a cheater bar) increases your leverage on the "twist," while a finer thread increases the "lift" of the screw itself.

Let's Put it to Work

Imagine you are using a Screw Jack to lift the corner of a heavy workbench so you can swap out the casters.

The Data:

Pitch (P): 0.25 inches (This means one full turn moves the jack up 1/4 of an inch).

Handle Length (R): 12 inches (The distance from the center of the screw to where you are pulling).

The Goal: What is the Mechanical Advantage (MA) of this jack?

The Solution:

The formula looks a bit fancy because of the circle, but don't let it scare you. You are comparing the distance your hand travels in one full circle (2×π×Radius) to how far the jack lifts (the Pitch).

MA= (2 × π × Radius) / Pitch

Using π ≈ 3.14:

Distance your hand moves: 2 × 3.14 × 12 inches = 75.36 inches.

Distance the load moves: 0.25 inches.

MA = 75.36/0.25 = 301.44

Answer: This jack has a Mechanical Advantage of roughly **301**. This means if you pull with just 10 pounds of force on that handle, the jack is pushing UP with over 3,000 pounds! That's why we use screws for the heaviest lifting.

Gears and Gear Trains

Gears and Gear Trains: Trading Speed for Power
A Gear Train is just a series of meshed gears that pass motion from one shaft to another. They are the ultimate "force multipliers."

The Golden Rule of Gears
There are two things you need to watch: Direction and Ratio.

The Direction Flip: Every time two gears touch (mesh), the direction flips. If the first gear goes clockwise, the second goes counter-clockwise.

The Size Swap: * Small Gear turning a Big Gear: You gain Torque (power) but lose Speed.

Big Gear turning a Small Gear: You gain Speed but lose Torque.

Brian's Pro Tip: Think of it like a bike. When you're going uphill, you want a small gear in the front and a big one in the back. You have to pedal a lot (speed), but it's much easier to push the bike up the hill (power).

Let's Put it to Work
Imagine we have three gears lined up on a bench: Gear A, Gear B, and Gear C.

The Data:

Gear A (The Driver): 20 teeth, turning Clockwise at 60 RPM.

Gear B (The Idler): 60 teeth.

Gear C (The Driven): 10 teeth.

The Goal: How fast is Gear C turning, and in which direction?

Step 1: Follow the Direction

Gear A is Clockwise.

Gear B (touching A) must flip to Counter-Clockwise.

Gear C (touching B) flips back to Clockwise.

Result: Gear C is turning Clockwise.

Step 2: Compare the Start to the Finish
Here's a secret: In a simple train like this, the middle gear (Gear B) is just an "Idler." It changes the direction, but it doesn't change the final speed ratio between the first and last gear. You can actually ignore it for the speed calculation!

Compare Gear A (20 teeth) directly to Gear C (10 teeth).

Ratio: 20 / 10 = 2.

Since Gear A is twice as big as Gear C, Gear C has to spin twice as fast to keep up.

The Calculation:

60 RPM (Gear A)×2=120 RPM
Answer: Gear C is turning at 120 RPM in a Clockwise direction.

Basic Physics

Understanding Energy: Potential, Kinetic, and Mechanical

In the trades, we don't just talk about energy in the abstract—we see it every time a hammer hits a nail or a truck rounds a corner. At its simplest, energy is the ability to do work.

1. Potential Energy: Energy on Standby
Think of potential energy as "stored" energy. It's the energy an object has because of its position or its condition.

Gravitational Potential Energy
This is the most common type you'll deal with. It's simply the energy an object has because it's been lifted off the ground. Gravity is pulling on it, just waiting for it to drop.

The formula we use is:

$$PE_{grav} = m \cdot g \cdot h$$

m = Mass (in kg)

g = Gravity (on Earth, this is always 9.8 m/s^2)

h = Height (in meters)

The Rule of Thumb: The higher you lift something, the more potential energy it has. If you lift a 1kg weight 5 meters, it has 49 Joules of energy. Double that height to 10 meters, and you double the energy to 98 Joules.

Elastic Potential Energy

This happens when you stretch or compress something out of its natural shape—like a spring, a bungee cord, or even a hockey stick during a slap shot.

To find this, we use the formula:

$PE_{elastic} = 1/2\ kx^2$

k = The "spring constant" (how stiff the material is)

x = The distance it's stretched or squished (in meters)

When a hockey player leans into a shot, the stick bends. That "bend" is elastic potential energy. When the stick snaps back, all that stored energy is dumped into the puck.

2. Kinetic Energy: Energy in Motion

Once an object starts moving, that potential energy turns into Kinetic Energy (KE).

The formula for Kinetic Energy is:

$KE = 1/2\ mv^2$

m = Mass (kg)

v = Velocity (meters per second)

The "Square" Warning: Notice that the velocity (v) is squared. This is why speed is so dangerous. If you double your speed, you don't double the energy—you quadruple it ($2^2 = 4$). If you go four times as fast, you have 16 times the energy ($4^2 = 16$).

This is why a small bullet or a fast-moving truck carries such a massive punch. They have "velocity on their side."

3. Mechanical Energy: The Total Package

In the real world, objects often have both potential and kinetic energy at the same time. We call the sum of these two Mechanical Energy.

Mechanical Energy = Potential Energy + Kinetic Energy

The Pole-Vaulter Example:
Think of a pole-vaulter in Victoria during a track meet.

The Run: She's sprinting (Kinetic Energy).

The Plant: She plants the pole and it bends (Elastic Potential Energy).

The Rise: As she rises into the air, she gains height (Gravitational Potential Energy).

Her total "Mechanical Energy" is the combination of her speed and the spring in that pole working together to get her over the bar.

Why This Matters for the Trades
Whether you are calculating the force needed for a crane to lift a load or understanding how a hydraulic press stores energy, these basics are what keep you—and the people around you—safe on the job site. We triple-check these formulas because, out in the field, "close enough" isn't good enough.

Work and Power: Getting the Job Done

In everyday life, we say we're "working" when we're at the shop or on-site. But in physics, Work has a very specific definition. If nothing moves, no work is being done. You could push against a brick wall until you're blue in the face, but if that wall doesn't budge, the "work" performed is zero.

1. What is Work?

Work happens when a force causes an object to move. We measure it in Joules (J). One Joule is the work done when 1 Newton of force moves an object 1 meter (J = Nm).

The formula we use is:

$W = F \cdot d \cdot \cos\theta$

W = Work (Joules)

F = Force (Newtons)

d = Distance (meters)

θ (Theta) = The angle between the direction you are pushing and the direction the object is actually moving.

The Three Ways Angle Affects Your Work:
The "Cosine" part sounds technical, but it really just boils down to three scenarios on the job:

Scenario A: Pushing in the same direction ($\theta=0°$). If you're pulling a tool cart and the cart moves exactly where you're pulling, you get full credit. $\cos 0° = 1$, so you just multiply Force × Distance.

Scenario B: Working against motion ($\theta=180°$). This is "negative work." Think of friction on a slide or brakes on a truck. The force is pointing one way, but the object is moving the other. It's hindering the movement.

Scenario C: The "Waitress" Trap ($\theta=90°$). This is the weird one. If you carry a heavy box across a level shop floor, you are applying upward force to keep it from falling, but the box is moving horizontally. Because your force is at a right angle to the movement, you are technically doing zero work to move it sideways. The truck carrying cargo across Canada does no "work" to keep the boxes in the bed—it only did work to lift them in there in the first place!

2. Power: How Fast Can You Do It?

If Work is about what you did, Power is about how fast you did it.

If two apprentices both carry ten bundles of shingles up a ladder, they've done the same amount of Work. But if one does it in five minutes and the other takes an hour, the first one used a lot more Power.

The formula for Power is:

$P = W/t$

P = Power (measured in Watts)

W = Work (Joules)

t = Time (seconds)

A Shortcut for the Trades
Sometimes we don't know the total work, but we know how much force we're applying and how fast we're going. Since Work is Force × Distance, and Distance/Time is Velocity, we can also use this:

Power = Force • Velocity

The Takeaway:

To get more Power, you either need to push harder (Force) or move faster (Velocity).

The less time it takes to do a job, the more Power is required. This is why a high-wattage motor can lift a load faster than a low-wattage one.

Defining Force and Newton's Three Laws

In the simplest terms, a Force is a push or a pull. It's what makes things move, stop, or change direction. We measure force in Newtons (N).

To give you an idea of what a Newton is: If you take a 1kg mass and accelerate it by 1 meter per second squared ($1m/s^2$), you've used exactly 1 Newton of force.

$1N = 1kg \cdot 1m/s^2$

1. The First Law: The Law of Inertia

"An object at rest stays at rest, and an object in motion stays in motion, unless a force acts on it."

In the trades, we call this "stubbornness." An object wants to keep doing exactly what it's already doing.

Mass is the Key: The more mass an object has, the more Inertia it has.

The Job Site Example: It's a lot easier to slide an empty toolbox across the floor than one full of heavy wrenches. The full box has more mass, so it has more "stubbornness" (inertia) against moving.

The "Space" Rule: If you threw a hammer in the vacuum of deep space, it would travel at the same speed in a straight line forever because there's no air friction or gravity to stop it.

2. The Second Law: The "F=ma" Rule

"Force equals mass times acceleration."

This law tells us exactly how much "push" we need to get something moving.

$F = m \cdot a$
F = Force (Newtons)
m = Mass (kg)
a = Acceleration (m/s^2)

The Practical Side: If you want to move a heavy piece of machinery (high mass) at a fast clip (high acceleration), you're going to need a massive amount of Force. This is why we use heavy-duty jacks and cranes for the big stuff—we're fighting the relationship between mass and the speed we want to achieve.

3. The Third Law: Action and Reaction

"For every action, there is an equal and opposite reaction."

This one is often the hardest to wrap your head around, but it's the reason your ladder stays leaning against a wall instead of falling through it.

The Table Example: If you set a heavy 10kg motor on a workbench, gravity is pulling that motor down. But the workbench is actually pushing up with the exact same amount of force.

Equilibrium: As long as those two forces are equal, the motor stays put. We call this Equilibrium.

The Snap: If the bench is poorly made and can only push back with half the force, it's going to snap. The "reaction" wasn't strong enough to match the "action."

The Hand-on-Desk Test: If you hit a desk with your hand, the desk hits you back with the same force. That's why your hand hurts—the desk isn't just sitting there; it's pushing back!

Friction: The Force That Holds Us Back

In the simplest terms, Friction is the resistance to motion. It's the force that happens when two surfaces rub together. Without it, you couldn't walk across a room, and your truck tires would just spin in place like they were on pure ice.

1. The Two Faces of Friction

In the trades, we generally look at friction in two states: Static (sitting still) and Kinetic (moving).

Static Friction (The "Sticking" Force)
This is the friction between two objects that are not moving relative to each other. It's what keeps your toolbox from sliding off the tailgate when you're parked on a hill.

The Grip: Static friction determines how much "push" is needed to get something started.

Angle of Repose: This is a fancy term for the steepest angle a surface can have before an object starts to slide. If you tilt a workbench, there is a specific angle where gravity finally wins and the book slides off. We calculate that with:

$$\tan\theta = \mu_s$$

(Where θ is the angle and μ_s is the "grippiness" of the surface).

Kinetic Friction (The "Slowing" Force)
Once an object starts sliding, you are dealing with Kinetic Friction. Interestingly, it usually takes more force to get an object moving (Static) than it does to keep it moving (Kinetic). This is why you have to give a heavy crate a big heave to start it, but then it slides a bit easier.

2. How We Calculate Friction
The formula looks a bit technical, but it's actually quite straightforward once you break it down:

$$f = \mu F_n$$

f = The Force of Friction.

μ (Mu) = The Coefficient of Friction. This is just a number that describes how "rough" or "smooth" the two surfaces are. Rubber on concrete has a high μ (lots of grip); ice on steel has a very low μ (very slippery).

F_n (Normal Force) = The force pushing the two surfaces together (usually the weight of the object).

3. The Rules of the Road (Amontons' Laws)
There are a few "common sense" rules about friction that often pop up on Canadian trade exams:

More weight = More friction: If you double the weight of a load, you double the friction. It's directly proportional.

Surface area doesn't change the friction: This one surprises people. Whether you slide a brick on its side or its face, the friction force is technically the same.

Speed doesn't change the friction: Whether you are sliding a board slowly or quickly, the kinetic friction resisting you stays pretty much the same.

Why This Matters for the Trades
At our Victoria office, we've seen how understanding friction saves lives. It's why we care about tire tread depth and why we use lubricants like oil or grease in engines to reduce friction where we don't want it. In the trades, you're either trying to create friction (brakes, grip) or get rid of it (bearings, sliding joints).

Knowing the difference between "staying put" and "sliding away" is what keeps a job site running safely.

Electromagnetism: Putting Electricity to Work

In its simplest form, electromagnetism is the relationship between an electric current and a magnetic field. For a tradesperson, it's the secret sauce that allows us to turn a flow of electrons into physical mechanical work.

1. The Coil and the Core

If you run electricity through a straight wire, it creates a tiny magnetic field around it. But if you wrap that wire into a coil, those little magnetic fields stack up and become powerful.

If you put a piece of iron (the core) inside that coil, you've just built an Electromagnet.

> **The Switch:** Unlike a permanent magnet on your fridge, an electromagnet can be turned on and off.

> **The Strength:** The more "juice" (current) you run through it, or the more times you wrap the wire, the stronger the magnet becomes.

2. The Right-Hand Rule

How do you know which way the magnetic field is spinning? We use a simple trick called the Right-Hand Rule.

> 1. Make a "thumbs up" with your right hand.
>
> 2. Your thumb points in the direction of the current flow (+ to −).
>
> 3. Your fingers curling around represent the direction of the magnetic field.

This helps you understand how the field will interact with other magnets or wires nearby—critical when you're wiring up motors or transformers.

3. Electromagnetism in Action
This principle is the "muscle" behind three of the most common components you'll see in the trades:

The Solenoid
A solenoid is basically a coil of wire with a movable iron rod (a plunger) inside it. When you "energize" the coil, the magnetic field sucks the rod into the center.

> **Use:** This linear motion is used to open valves (like in a dishwasher) or engage a starter motor in a truck.

The Relay
A relay is just an electromagnetic switch. You use a small, safe amount of current to energize a coil. That coil becomes a magnet and pulls a set of heavy-duty contacts closed.

> **Use:** This allows a tiny dashboard switch to turn on a massive, power-hungry piece of equipment without melting the switch in your hand.

The Electric Motor
A motor uses electromagnetism to create rotation. By placing a coil of wire inside a set of permanent magnets and running current through it, the magnetic fields "push" against each other.

The Result: Since the magnets are fixed and the coil is on a shaft, the coil has nowhere to go but around. That's how we turn "juice" into a spinning drill or a table saw.

4. The Inverse Square Law
Just like the heat from a woodstove, the power of a magnet drops off fast as you move away. If you double the distance from an electromagnet, the force doesn't just cut in half—it drops to one-quarter ($1/2^2$). In the shop, this means your solenoids and relays have to be designed so the parts are very close together to work effectively.

Why It Matters
At my kitchen table in Victoria, I always tell students: electricity isn't just about lighting bulbs; it's about motion. Whether it's a "clunk" from a solenoid or the "whir" of a motor, you're seeing electromagnetism in action. We triple-check these basics because once you understand the coil and the core, the rest of the electrical world starts to make a whole lot of sense.

Gravity: The Heavy Lifter

In the simplest terms, Gravity is the pull between two objects. On Earth, it's the force that pulls everything toward the center of the planet at a constant acceleration of 9.8 m/s^2.

For a trades person, gravity isn't just a theory—it's the weight you have to lift, the load you have to balance, and the reason things fall.

1. Mass vs. Weight (Know the Difference)
In common speech, we use these words interchangeably, but for your trade exam, they are very different.

> **Mass:** This is the amount of "stuff" or matter in an object. It is measured in kilograms (kg). Your mass never changes—whether you're in Victoria or on the Moon, a 10kg motor still has 10kg of mass.

> **Weight:** This is a force. It is the pull of gravity on that mass. It is measured in Newtons (N).

The formula for weight is:

Weight = Mass · Gravity

If you have a 100kg crate, its weight on Earth is roughly 980 Newtons (100 · 9.8). If you took that same crate to the Moon, it would still be 100kg, but it would feel much lighter because the "pull" is weaker.

2. The Center of Gravity (The "Tipping Point")

This is the most critical concept for safety. The Center of Gravity (CG) is the single point where the entire weight of an object is concentrated.

> **Balance:** If you support an object directly under its CG, it will balance perfectly.

> **The Rule of Stability:** An object will stay upright as long as its Center of Gravity stays inside its base of support.

> **The Danger Zone:** As soon as the CG moves outside that base (like a forklift carrying a load too high or a person leaning too far off a ladder), gravity stops holding the object down and starts pulling it over.

3. Gravity and the Inverse Square Law

Gravity gets weaker the farther you move away from the center of the Earth. It follows the Inverse Square Law.

If you move x times farther away, the force of gravity drops to $1/x^2$.

If you move 2 times farther away, gravity is 1/4 as strong ($2^2 = 4$).

If you move 10 times farther away, gravity is 1/100 as strong ($10^2 = 100$).

For most trade work, we treat gravity as a constant 9.8 m/s^2, but this law explains why satellites stay in orbit—they are far enough away that the "pull" is balanced by their speed.

Why This Matters for the Trades

At our shop, we've spent years "triple-checking" safety tutorials because we know the stakes.

> **Crane Operators:** Need to know the CG of a load to rig it level.

Forklift Drivers: Need to know how raising a load shifts the CG forward, risking a tip-over.

Carpenters: Need to know how to set the base of a ladder so the CG of the person climbing stays safely between the rails.

Gravity is a predictable partner if you respect the Center of Gravity. If you don't, it's a force that never misses an opportunity to pull things toward the dirt.

The Four States of Matter

In the trades, we look at matter based on how much the molecules are "holding onto" each other.

1. Solids: The Rigid Structure
In a solid, molecules are locked tight. They vibrate, but they don't move past each other.

Polycrystalline (Metals/Ice): These have a neat, repeating lattice structure. This is why metals conduct heat and electricity so well—the "grid" allows energy to move through easily.

Amorphous (Plastics/Glass): These are a jumbled mess of molecules. They don't have a specific melting point; they just get softer and "goopy" as you heat them.

2. Liquids: The Unstoppable Fluid
When you add enough heat, those rigid bonds break. The molecules stay close (density remains high), but they can now slide past each other.

Hydraulics Rule: Liquids are incompressible. This is vital. Because the molecules are already touching, you can't squish them closer. This allows a brake pedal in the cab to move a heavy caliper at the wheel instantly.

Viscosity: This is a liquid's "thickness" or resistance to flow. As a mechanic, you know that cold oil is thick (high viscosity) and hot oil is thin (low viscosity).

3. Gases: The Expandable Fluid

Add even more heat, and the molecules fly apart completely. They have no fixed shape or volume.

Compression: Unlike liquids, gases are compressible. You can shove a lot of air into a small compressor tank because there is mostly empty space between the molecules.

Pressure & Temperature: If you squeeze a gas into a smaller space (increasing pressure), it gets hot. If you let it expand quickly, it gets cold. This is exactly how a refrigerator or AC unit works.

4. Plasma: The "Arc" State

Plasma is super-heated gas where the electrons are ripped away from the atoms.

The Trade Connection: You see this every time you use a Plasma Cutter or an Arc Welder. The "spark" is actually a path of plasma that conducts electricity to melt metal.

Phase Changes: Boiling, Freezing, and Pressure

The most important thing for the trades is the "Transition Point"—where matter jumps from one state to another.

The Soldering Example (Solid to Liquid)

When you solder a copper pipe, you are looking for the Melting Point. You heat the joint until the solid solder turns into a liquid. Because it's a liquid, it uses "capillary action" to suck itself into the fitting before it cools back into a solid.

The Refrigerant Secret (Pressure vs. Boiling)
Most people think water only boils at 100°C. But that's only at sea level.

> **Lower the Pressure:** If you put a vacuum pump on a line, you lower the pressure. Water will then boil at room temperature! This is how HVAC techs "evacuate" a system—they boil off moisture without using a torch.

> **Raise the Pressure:** If you increase the pressure, you raise the boiling point. This is why your car's radiator is pressurized; it keeps the coolant from boiling even when the engine is way over 100°C.

Why This Matters
At our shop in Victoria, we've seen plenty of folks get confused by "slugging" a compressor (trying to compress liquid refrigerant) or failing to get a good solder flow. It all comes back to these basics. If you know how pressure and heat change the state of your materials, you'll be the one fixing the problems others can't see.

Heat Transfer: The Three Ways Energy Moves

There are only three ways heat can travel. Understanding the difference is what makes you an expert at keeping a building warm or a weld strong.

1. Conduction: The "Hand-to-Hand" Pass
Conduction is heat moving through a solid object by direct contact. Think of it like a bucket brigade—the molecules don't move from one end to the other, they just vibrate and pass the energy to their neighbor.

> **The Trade Connection:** This is why a copper pipe gets hot way down the line when you're soldering one end. Copper is a "conductor" because its molecules are great at passing that energy along.

> **The Insulator:** Materials like fiberglass or spray foam are "poor conductors." We use them to slow down conduction so the heat stays inside the house during a Victoria winter.

2. Convection: The "Current" Move

Convection is heat moving through fluids (which, in physics, means both liquids and gases). As a fluid gets hot, it expands, becomes less dense, and rises. Cooler, denser fluid sinks to take its place, creating a "convection current."

> **The Trade Connection:** This is how a forced-air furnace works. It heats the air, which then circulates through the house. It's also why a plumber needs to understand how hot water rises in a tank—if you don't get the circulation right, the top of the tank is scalding while the bottom is freezing.
>
> **HVAC Tip:** We use fans to create "forced convection," pushing the air exactly where we want it instead of waiting for nature to do it.

3. Radiation: The "Invisible" Wave

Radiation is heat moving through electromagnetic waves. It doesn't need a solid or a fluid to travel—it can go through a vacuum (like the sun's heat reaching Earth).

> **The Trade Connection:** If you've ever felt the heat coming off a glowing red weld before you even touch it, that's radiation.
>
> **Radiant Heating:** Many modern homes in BC use "radiant floor heating." We pump hot water through tubes in the floor, and that heat radiates upward, warming the objects and people in the room directly rather than just heating the air.

The Laws of Thermodynamics (The Rules of the Game)

There are two main "laws" that you'll see pop up on your Canadian Red Seal or entrance exams:

The First Law: Conservation of Energy

Energy cannot be created or destroyed—it only changes form.

In the Shop: When you use an electric heater, you aren't "making" energy; you're converting electrical energy into heat energy. In a car engine, you're converting chemical energy (fuel) into heat and motion.

The Second Law: The "One-Way Street"

Heat always flows from a higher temperature to a lower temperature.

The Practical Side: A "heat pump" doesn't actually create heat. It uses a refrigerant cycle to "trick" the second law, grabbing the small amount of heat in the outside air and pumping it into your warm house. It takes work (electricity) to move heat "uphill" against this law.

Why This Matters

At our office, we've spent years triple-checking these tutorials because we know that understanding heat is about more than just comfort—it's about efficiency and safety.

Welders: Need to know how conduction will warp a plate.

Plumbers: Need to know how thermal expansion (heat making things grow) can snap a pipe if there's no room for it to move.

HVAC Techs: Spend their whole lives balancing these three forces to keep a system running.

If you can master where the heat is going, you've mastered half the job.

The Golden Rule: Liquids Don't Squish

If you take a jar full of hydraulic oil and try to jam a lid down into it, it won't budge. This is because liquids are incompressible.

1. Hydraulics (The Heavy Lifters)
Because you can't "squish" oil, it acts like a solid steel rod. If you push one end of a hydraulic line, the other end moves instantly.

> **The Power:** Since the liquid doesn't absorb any of the energy by compressing, almost 100% of the force you apply at the pump goes straight to the cylinder.

> **The Danger:** Because oil doesn't squish, if a line blocks or a valve fails, the pressure builds up instantly until something snaps. This is why we triple-check our relief valves.

The Bouncy Rule: Gases Do Squish
Gases, like the air in a pneumatic system, have a lot of "empty space" between the molecules. When you apply pressure, they crowd together. We say gases are compressible.

2. Pneumatics (The Fast Workers)
Think of air like a big, invisible spring.

> **The Cushion:** Because air squishes, pneumatic tools (like a nail gun or an air-ride seat) have a "bounce" to them. This protects the tool from shattering and makes for a smoother ride in a truck.

> **The Storage:** You can "pack" a huge amount of air into a small tank. You can't do that with oil. This stored energy is why an air tank can still run a tool even after you turn the compressor off.

Pascal's Law: The Tradesman's Best Friend

This is the most important rule for your exam. Blaise Pascal figured out that pressure applied to an enclosed fluid is transmitted equally in all directions.

If you have a closed system—like the brake lines in a car—and you push on one end, that pressure doesn't just go to one wheel; it hits every square inch of the system with the exact same force.

Mechanical Advantage (The "Magic" of Hydraulics)

This law allows us to trade distance for force.

If you push a small piston down a long way, you can move a massive piston a short way.

It's exactly like a lever, but using fluid instead of a board. This is how a small person can lift a 20-ton house with a hydraulic jack.

Pressure vs. Flow: Don't Get Them Confused

In the shop, we see folks mix these up all the time:

> **Pressure is Force:** Pressure is what gives you the "grunt" to lift the load. It's measured in PSI (Pounds per Square Inch) or kPa.

> **Flow is Speed:** Flow is how much fluid is moving. It's measured in GPM (Gallons Per Minute). If the bucket on your backhoe is moving too slowly, you need more flow. If it can't lift the rock at all, you need more pressure.

Why This Matters

At our Victoria office, we always emphasize safety with pressure. A pinhole leak in a hydraulic line at 3,000 PSI isn't just a mess—it can cut through a leather glove and inject oil right into your skin.

Understanding that "liquids don't squish" tells you why hydraulic systems are so rigid and powerful, while knowing "gases do squish" helps you understand why air systems need tanks and why they feel "spongy."

Flashpoint: The "Match" Test

The Flashpoint is the lowest temperature at which a liquid gives off enough vapour to ignite in the air when a flame is present.

Think of it this way: the liquid itself doesn't usually burn—the vapour sitting on top of it does.

> **Flammable Liquids (Danger):** These have a flashpoint below 37.8°C. Since room temperature is usually around 20°C, these are "ready to go." If you spill gasoline, it is already "off-gassing" enough vapour to catch fire from a single spark.

> **Combustible Liquids:** These have a flashpoint above 37.8°C. They are safer to store, but once they get hot (like hydraulic oil in a running machine), they become just as dangerous as gas.

2. The Fire Triangle

For a fire to happen on your job site, you need three things. Take one away, and the fire dies.

> **Fuel:** The stuff that burns (lumber, solvent, oily rags).

> **Heat:** The "trigger" (a spark, a cigarette, a hot pipe).

> **Oxygen:** It's in the air all around us.

The Shop Tip: Oily rags can actually create their own heat through a chemical reaction (spontaneous combustion). We always put them in a sealed metal bin to starve them of Oxygen.

3. WHMIS 2015: The "Silent Language"

WHMIS (Workplace Hazardous Materials Information System) is how we label the "bad stuff" so you don't have to guess. Since 2015, we've used the GHS (Globally Harmonized System), which means the symbols are the same whether you're in Victoria or Vancouver.

The Big Three You'll See Most:

The Flame: This means the stuff has a low flashpoint. Keep it away from the "Heat" part of the triangle.

> **The Skull and Crossbones:** This is "Acute Toxicity." It can kill you fast if you breathe it in or get it on your skin.

> **The Exclamation Mark:** This is for "lesser" hazards—it might give you a rash, make you dizzy, or irritate your lungs.

4. The SDS (Your Best Friend)

Every chemical on your site must have a Safety Data Sheet (SDS). Don't let "Big Prep" fool you—you don't need to memorize the whole sheet, but you do need to know where to find Section 4 (First Aid) and Section 9 (Physical Properties).

Section 9 is where you find that Flashpoint. If it says "Flashpoint: -40°C," you know that even in a Victoria winter, that stuff is ready to blow.

Why This Matters

At our kitchen table, we've triple-checked these safety rules because we want every "forgotten" student to make it home at the end of the shift. Knowing why a solvent catches fire at room temperature isn't just "chemistry"—it's the difference between a normal day and a trip to the burn unit.

If you see a "Flame" pictogram, check the flashpoint. If it's lower than the temperature in your shop, you're working in a powder keg.

The Launchpad: Reading Self-Assessment & Strategy

Before we dive into the nuts and bolts of the TEE, we need to see where you're standing. Think of this chapter as a quick tune-up for your brain. We've put together a set of tutorials to brush up on the basics, followed by a self-assessment that mirrors the hurdles you'll face on the actual exam.

I want to be clear: these aren't the exact questions you'll see on test day. Anyone who claims they have the "real" questions is probably trying to sell you a bridge in Vancouver. The TEE changes all the time, and quite frankly, memorizing old questions won't help you when the pressure is on. Instead, we've spent years in the classroom and at the drafting table making sure these practice sets build the skills you need to handle whatever the examiners throw at you.

We're using this self-assessment to:

Spot the gaps: Find out exactly where you're solid and where you're tripping up.

Build your roadmap: Use your results to focus your study time where it actually matters.

Get comfortable: Shake off the pre-test jitters by getting used to the TEE's rhythm and style.

Bonus Practice: This assessment is beefy—it's essentially a third practice test tucked into your study guide.

This isn't a full-blown university course; we're assuming you've read a blueprint or a manual once or twice. But if you find some of this tricky, don't sweat it. That just means it's time to slow down or maybe find a bit of extra help.

The goal here is to give you a baseline score. Once you finish, look at the table below to see how you stack up and what your next move should be.

Scoring Guide: Where Do You Stand?

Score Range	What it Means	Your Next Step
80% - 100%	You've got a sharp eye for detail.	Focus on your weaker subjects; just do a light review here.
60% - 79%	You're on the right track, but missing the finer points.	Go through the tutorials again and practice active reading.
Below 60%	This area is going to be a struggle on exam day.	Dig deep into the tutorials and consider extra reading exercises.

Reading Self-Assessment

	A	B	C	D
1	○	○	○	○
2	○	○	○	○
3	○	○	○	○
4	○	○	○	○
5	○	○	○	○
6	○	○	○	○
7	○	○	○	○
8	○	○	○	○
9	○	○	○	○
10	○	○	○	○
11	○	○	○	○
12	○	○	○	○
13	○	○	○	○
14	○	○	○	○
15	○	○	○	○
16	○	○	○	○
17	○	○	○	○
18	○	○	○	○
19	○	○	○	○
20	○	○	○	○

Passage 1: Instruction Manual (Electrical)
Before installing the new ceiling fan model #CF-700, ensure the main breaker to the circuit is in the OFF position. Attach the mounting bracket to the junction box using two 1/2-inch wood screws. The bracket must be able to support a minimum of 50 pounds. Connect the green ground wire from the bracket to the bare copper wire in the junction box. Next, connect the white neutral wires and the black hot wires, securing each connection with a wire nut and a wrap of electrical tape. Failure to correctly attach the ground wire could result in an electrical shock hazard. The fan blades should be attached after the motor housing is securely fastened to the mounting bracket.

1. According to the passage, what is the first step a technician must take before beginning the installation?

    a. Attach the fan blades.

    b. Connect the wires.

    c. Turn the main breaker to the OFF position.

    d. Secure the motor housing.

2. Which pair of wires must be connected to ensure the fan is properly grounded?

    a. The black wire and the white wire.

    b. The green wire and the bare copper wire.

    c. The 1/2-inch wood screws.

    d. The wire nut and electrical tape.

3. How much weight must the mounting bracket be capable of supporting?

    a. Exactly 1/2-inch.

    b. More than 700 pounds.

    c. A minimum of 50 pounds.

    d. Up to two wood screws.

4. What is the potential hazard mentioned if the ground wire is not correctly attached?

    a. The fan will spin too fast.

    b. The wire nut will fall off.

    c. An electrical shock hazard.

    d. The mounting bracket will fail.

Passage 2: Safety Data Sheet (SDS) - Section 7 (Welding Flux)

SDS Section 7: Handling and Storage
Precautions for Safe Handling: Avoid breathing dust/fume/gas/mist/vapors/spray. Do not eat, drink, or smoke when using this product. Use only outdoors or in a well-ventilated area.
Always wear appropriate Personal Protective Equipment (PPE), including safety glasses and leather welding gloves. **Wash thoroughly after handling.**

Conditions for Safe Storage, including any Incompatibilities: Store in a dry, cool, and well-ventilated place. Keep container tightly closed when not in use. Store away from oxidizing agents and strong acids. Keep out of reach of children. The recommended maximum storage temperature is **25° C 77° F** .

5. What temperature is the recommended maximum for storing this welding flux?

    a. Exactly 77° F}.

    b. 25° C or 77° F.

    c. Above 25° C.

    d. A dry, cool temperature.

6. What necessary action is specified to be done *after* **handling the product?**

    a. Store it away from strong acids.

    b., Keep the container tightly closed.

    c. Wash thoroughly.

    d. Put on safety glasses and gloves.

7. Which of the following conditions is incompatible with the safe storage of the welding flux?

    a. A dry and cool place.

    b. Storing away from strong acids.

    c. Storage near an oxidizing agent.

    d. Keeping the container tightly closed.

8. If a welder is working indoors with this product, what is the required condition for the work area?

    a. It must be 25° C.

    b. Eating and drinking are permitted.

    c. It must be a well-ventilated area.

    d. Welding gloves are optional.

Passage 3: Technical Specifications (Automotive)

The Model 4500 engine requires a specific type of synthetic oil to maintain optimal performance. The oil viscosity rating must be **5W-30** for year-round use. The oil filter should be a high-flow, premium spin-on type, specifically **Part Number XZ-2049**. The recommended oil change interval is **15,000 km** or once every **12 months**, whichever comes first. Exceeding the oil change interval risks premature wear on the crankshaft bearings. Furthermore, the spark plugs must be torqued to **28 Newton-metres (N•m** and replaced every 60,000 km}.

9. What is the specified viscosity rating for the synthetic oil used in the Model 4500 engine?

    a. 12 months.

    b. 5W-30.

    c. 28 N•m.

    d. Part Number XZ-2049.

10. A mechanic last changed the oil 11 months ago, and the vehicle has been driven 16,500 km} since then. Should the oil be changed now?

    a. No, because it hasn't been 12 months yet.

    b. Yes, because 16,500 km exceeds the 15,000 km} limit.

    c. Yes, because the spark plugs are due for replacement.

    d. No, because the 60,000 km} interval is much longer.

11. What component risks premature wear if the oil change interval is exceeded?

    a. The oil filter (Part Number XZ-2049).

    b. The spark plugs.

    c. The crankshaft bearings.

    d. The synthetic oil.

12. To what torque specification must the spark plugs be tightened?

    a. 15,000 km}.

    b. 60,000 km}.

    c. $5\text{W}-30$.

    d. $28 \text{ N}\cdot\text{m}$.

Passage 4: Site Safety Procedure (Construction)

All workers must attend a **mandatory safety orientation** before accessing the high-rise structure under construction. **Hard hats, steel-toed boots, and high-visibility vests** are required in all areas of the site, including the temporary office trailers. Scaffolding is to be inspected daily by a **competent person**, and the inspection log must be signed and dated.
A fall arrest system, including a full-body harness, lanyard, and anchor point, is required for any work performed at a height of **three metres (10 feet)** or greater. Personal cell phone use is strictly prohibited while operating machinery or working at height.

13. Which areas of the site require workers to wear a hard hat, steel-toed boots, and a high-visibility vest?

    a. Only on the scaffolding.

    b. Only when operating machinery.

    c. All areas, including the temporary office trailers.

    d. Only the high-rise structure itself.

14. What is the minimum height that requires a worker to use a fall arrest system?

    a. 10 feet 3 metres or greater.

    b. Any height where scaffolding is used.

    c. Only when operating machinery.

    d. The height of the temporary office trailers.

15. Who is responsible for the daily inspection of the scaffolding?

    a. The worker using the scaffolding.

    b. All workers on site.

    c. A competent person.

    d. The site safety officer only.

16. The safety procedure strictly prohibits personal cell phone use during which activities?

    A. Attending the mandatory safety orientation.

    B) Any time a worker is on site.

    C) Operating machinery or working at height.

    D) Daily scaffolding inspections.

Passage 5: Technical Drawing Note (Plumbing/HVAC)

NOTE 6: Pipe Insulation Schedule
All domestic hot water (DHW) supply and return piping running through unconditioned spaces (e.g., crawl spaces, exterior walls) shall be insulated with 1-inch thick, closed-cell elastomeric foam insulation. The minimum required R-value for this insulation is R-4. Cold water lines (CW) in the same areas must also be insulated, but only 3/4-inch thick insulation is required to prevent condensation, with a minimum R-value of R-3. All pipe joints, fittings, and valves must be completely covered with the same insulation material, sealed with an approved foil-backed tape.

17. What is the purpose of insulating the cold water lines (CW) in unconditioned spaces?

    a. To maintain the temperature of the cold water.

    b. To achieve a maximum R-4 value.

    c. To prevent condensation.

    d. To ensure the pipe is 1/4-inch thick.

18. What is the minimum R-value required for the insulation on the domestic hot water (DHW) supply lines?

    a. R-3.

    b. 3/4-inch}.

    c. R-4.

    d., 1-inch.

19. What is required to completely cover the pipe joints and fittings?

    a.. Foil-backed tape only.

    b. The same insulation material sealed with foil-backed tape.

    c. 3/4-inch insulation only.

    d. Closed-cell elastomeric foam.

20. How thick must the closed-cell elastomeric foam insulation be for the DHW supply piping?

    a. 3/4-inch.

    b. R-4.

    c. 1/4-inch.

    d. 1-inch.

Answers and Analysis

1. C
The passage states, "Before installing... ensure the main breaker... is in the OFF position." This is the mandatory first step.

2. B
The passage says to "Connect the green ground wire from the bracket to the bare copper wire in the junction box."

3. C
The passage specifies, "The bracket must be able to support a minimum of 50 pounds."

4. C
The text explicitly warns, "Failure to correctly attach the ground wire could result in an electrical shock hazard."

Passage 2: Safety Data Sheet (SDS) - Section 7 (Welding Flux)

5. B
The passage states, "The recommended maximum storage temperature is 25° C 77° F ."

6. C
The instructions for safe handling conclude with the instruction, "Wash thoroughly after handling."

7. C
The storage conditions list storing "away from oxidizing agents and strong acids." Storing near them is an incompatibility.

8. C
The safety precaution advises to "Use only outdoors or in a well-ventilated area," and this applies to indoor use as well.

Passage 3: Technical Specifications (Automotive)

9. B
The specifications clearly state, "The oil viscosity rating must be 5W-30."

10. B
The oil change interval is "15,000 km or once every 12 months, whichever comes first." Since 16,500 km} has been driven, the oil must be changed.

11. C
The passage warns, "Exceeding the oil change interval risks premature wear on the crankshaft bearings."

12. D
The passage states that spark plugs must be torqued to "28 Newton-metres N•m."

Passage 4: Site Safety Procedure (Construction)

13. C
The rule states PPE is required in "all areas of the site, including the temporary office trailers."

14. A
A fall arrest system is required for "any work performed at a height of three metres (10 feet) or greater."

15. C
The procedure specifies, "Scaffolding is to be inspected daily by a competent person."

16. C
Personal cell phone use is "strictly prohibited while operating machinery or working at height."

17. C
The passage states, "Cold water lines... must also be insulated... to prevent condensation."

18. C
The note specifies, "The minimum required R-value for this insulation is R-4" for the DHW piping.

19. B
The requirement is: "All pipe joints, fittings, and valves must be completely covered with the same insulation material, sealed with an approved foil-backed tape."

20. D
The DHW piping requires 1-inch thick insulation, as noted in the first sentence.

Reading on the Job: A Guide for the Trades

When you're out on a job site in the Pacific Northwest, nobody is going to hand you a 10-page essay on the history of architecture. Instead, you'll be staring at a Work Order, a Safety Data Sheet (SDS), or a confusing page from the Canadian Electrical Code.

"Big Prep" companies love to teach you how to analyze Shakespeare, but around here, we care about whether you can read a site report and not trip over a regulation. Here is how to tackle technical reading without losing your mind—or your afternoon.

1. Treat It Like a Tool, Not a Book
In the trades, we don't read for "pleasure"; we read for information.

Skip the fluff: If you have five different documents, start with the one you know best (like a familiar blueprint or a tool manual).

No "Speed-Reading": This isn't a race. If you misread a decimal point on a load-bearing calculation, a "fast" read becomes a very "expensive" mistake.

Read the Question First: Unlike an English lit class, in technical testing, I actually recommend looking at the question or the specific data point you need before diving into a massive table or manual. It gives your brain a "search term" to look for.

2. Know Your "Site Documents"
On a certification exam or a real-world site, you'll run into these specific types of questions. We've moved past "Main Idea" and into "Operational Reality":

Question Type	What they are really asking
Document Use	Can you find the boiling point of a chemical on an SDS?
Technical Lookup	Can you find the specific clearance rule in a Building Code index?
Site Reporting	Based on the supervisor's log, what time did the concrete pour start?
Inference	If the gauge is in the "red" zone, what is the logical next step for the operator?
Safety/Compliance	Which PPE is mandatory according to the warning labels provided?

3. Finding the "Main Point" (The Site Report)

In an essay, the "Main Idea" is a thesis. In the trades, the "Main Idea" is the Objective.

If you are reading a site report, ask yourself: "What is the one thing the foreman wants me to do or know?"

The Topic: Usually found in the header (e.g., "Daily Progress Report - Johnson Bridge").

The Action: Usually found in the "Comments" or "Action Items" section at the bottom.

Brian's Tip: If you're looking at a paragraph about a new safety regulation, the first sentence usually tells you what changed, and the last sentence tells you when it starts. Ignore the middle part until you've got those two nailed down.

4. Reading Tables and Graphs (The "Sea of Text")

Big Prep ignores charts, but for us, they are bread and butter. When you see a table:

Read the Title: What is this measuring? (e.g., "Voltage Drop over Distance").

Check the Units: Are we talking millimeters or inches? Volts or Amps?

Find the Intersection: Use your finger or a pen to track the row and column. Don't eyeball it; that's how mistakes happen in the rain at 4:00 PM.

5. Drawing Inferences on Site

An "inference" is just a fancy word for "situational awareness."

Example: You see a photo of a ladder leaning against a gutter with no one holding the base and the feet on uneven gravel.

The Inference: That's a safety violation waiting to happen. The text doesn't have to say "This is dangerous" for you to conclude that the worker needs to reset.

The "Strict Information" Rule: On a test, only use what is on the page. You might know a "better" way to wire a house because you've done it for ten years, but if the test passage says to use a specific (even if outdated) method, answer based on the text. Don't let your expertise get in the way of a correct answer.

6. Practice Like You Work

We've spent years in the classroom and at the kitchen table refining these questions to make sure they actually look like what you'll see on the Canadian Red Seal or provincial exams.

Underline the "Musts": When a manual says "The installer must...", underline it. That's a test question 90% of the time.

Cross Out the "Distractors": If an answer choice mentions "Global Synergy" or "Optimization," it's probably corporate junk. Toss it.

Reading for the trades is about being a detective. You're looking for the clues that let you get the job done right, safely, and on time.

The Bottom Line: Identifying the Primary Objective

In the trades, "The Big Picture" isn't just an academic concept—it's the difference between a job well done and a costly (or dangerous) mistake. Whether you are looking at a work order, a safety bulletin, or an apprenticeship exam question, you need to be able to look at a wall of text and figure out the **Primary Objective**.

Think of it like being handed a complex blueprint. You don't start by counting every screw; you look at the title block and the main drawing to see what you're actually building. That is "Main Idea" in a nutshell.

Why "The Bottom Line" Matters
The "Big Prep" companies will tell you to look for "topic sentences" and "supporting details." Around here, we keep it simpler. On a job site, if the foreman gives you a three-minute explanation, you need to walk away knowing the one thing that *must* happen. On the exam, the test-writers are checking to see if you can separate the **core instruction** from the **background noise**.

How to Spot the Primary Objective
When you're staring at a paragraph on the exam, ask yourself these three "kitchen table" questions:

1. **Who is the "Boss" of this paragraph?** Usually, one sentence is doing the heavy lifting, while the others are just helping out.

2. **What is the "Call to Action"?** Is the text telling you how to maintain a tool, why a safety rule changed, or how to calculate a load?
3. **The "Elevator Pitch" Test:** If you had 10 seconds to tell your journeyman what this paragraph was about, what would you say?

Example: The "Safety First" Scenario
"Before operating the hydraulic shear, ensure the workspace is clear of debris. Check that the safety guards are locked in the 'down' position and verify that the emergency stop button is unobstructed. While regular maintenance of the blade is important for longevity, the immediate priority for any operator is ensuring that all secondary personnel remain behind the yellow safety line during the initiation sequence."

What is the Bottom Line (Main Idea)?

A) How to maintain a hydraulic blade.
B) The importance of clearing debris.
C) Ensuring safety protocols are met before starting the machine.
D) Keeping the emergency stop button clear.

All of those things are mentioned, but C is the "Boss." Maintenance (A) is for later; debris (B) and the stop button (D) are just parts of the overall safety protocol (C).

Tips for the Exam

> **Avoid the "Detail Trap":** Test-writers love to take a tiny detail from the second sentence and make it an answer choice. Just because it's true doesn't mean it's the Main Idea.
>
> **Check the First and Last:** In technical writing, the Primary Objective is often tucked into the very first or very last sentence.
>
> **Look for "Pivot" Words:** Words like However, Ultimately, or Above all are like a flashing neon sign pointing right at the Bottom Line.

By practicing this, you'll stop seeing a paragraph as a hurdle and start seeing it as a set of instructions. You're not just passing a test; you're making sure that when you get out there on the tools, you're the person who always knows exactly what the goal is.

Reading Between the Lines: Technical Troubleshooting

In the trades, we don't always get a step-by-step "how-to" guide for every situation. Often, a journeyman or a manual will give you a set of facts, and they expect you to have the common sense to figure out what comes next. On the entrance exam, "Drawing Inferences" is just a fancy way of testing your Technical Troubleshooting skills.

It's about taking the evidence on the page and "predicting the next step" before something goes sideways.

What is an Inference on the Job Site?
An inference is a conclusion you reach based on evidence and reasoning. It isn't explicitly written in the text, but the facts point directly to it.
If you walk into a shop and see a puddle of oil under a compressor and a "Caution" tag on the power switch, nobody has to tell you the machine is leaking and shouldn't be turned on. You've just "inferred" the situation.

How to Troubleshoot the Text
When you're faced with a "Reading Between the Lines" question, follow this simple process:

> **Gather the Facts:** List exactly what the text tells you. (e.g., "The gauge is in the red" and "The bypass is open.")
>
> **Apply Trade Logic:** What do those facts usually mean in the real world? (Red usually means danger/overload; a bypass means the main system couldn't handle the flow.)

Predict the Outcome: Based on those two things, what is the most likely reality? (The system is failing or under extreme stress.)

Example: The "Site Conditions" Scenario

"The forecast for the Fort McMurray job site calls for temperatures to drop below -30°C tonight. The site supervisor has issued a memo stating that all diesel equipment not currently in the heated bay must be plugged into the external heater blocks by 4:00 PM. No exceptions will be made for the morning shift start-up at 6:00 AM."

What can be concluded (inferred) from this memo?

A) The morning shift starts too early.

B) Diesel engines may fail to start in extreme cold without pre-heating.

C) The heated bay is currently empty and ready for equipment.

D) The site supervisor is concerned about the cost of electricity.

The text doesn't say diesel engines won't start (B). However, because we know it's freezing and the "Bottom Line" is to plug them in or there are "no exceptions" for the morning start, we can infer that the equipment won't turn over if it stays cold. That's your troubleshooting skill at work.

Tips for Success

Stick to the Evidence: An inference must be supported by the text. Don't let your imagination run wild. If the text doesn't mention the "cost of electricity," don't pick an answer about the budget.

Watch for "Cause and Effect": If the text describes a cause (a heavy load) and a symptom (a grinding noise), the inference is almost always the effect (the bearing is likely failing).

Look for "Missing" Instructions: If a manual says "Step 1: Shut off power" and "Step 3: Replace the fuse," you can infer that Step 2 involves opening the panel.

At the end of the day, the exam isn't trying to trick you with riddles. They want to see if you're the kind of person who sees the "pressure in the red" and knows exactly what it means for the rest of the crew.

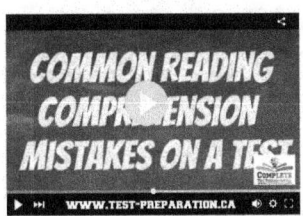

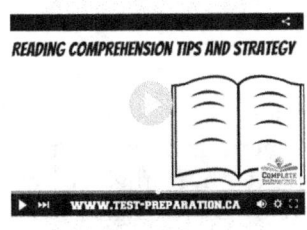

English Essentials: Finding Your Starting Line

This part of the book is here to help you get your bearings. Inside, you'll find a self-assessment to see where you stand, along with some straightforward tutorials to brush up on the basics.

We aren't trying to replace a full high school English credit here. We assume you've got the fundamentals down, but if any of these tutorials feel like pulling teeth, it might be a good sign to grab some extra help outside these pages. Remember, we've built these questions to sharpen your skills—they aren't carbon copies of the exam, but they hit the same nerves.

What's on the Menu?
To give you a clear look at what the TEE usually throws at you, we've focused on the core "building blocks" of the language:

Grammar & Usage: Putting the right words in the right order.

Vocabulary: Understanding meaning based on the "neighborhood" of the sentence.

The Details: Spelling, Punctuation, and Capitalization.

Sentence Structure: How it all hangs together.

A quick heads-up: The folks who run the TEE like to move the goalposts. They swap out questions, change the timing, or tweak the formats every year. We don't have a crystal ball, and frankly, if we gave you the exact questions, you wouldn't actually be learning. But here's the good news: if you can handle the "heavy lifting" in this section, you'll be ready for whatever they throw at you on test day.

Using the Self-Assessment

Think of this assessment as a "diagnostic run" for your brain. It's designed to:

Spot the areas where you're already a pro and where you're a bit rusty.

Help you build a study plan that actually fits your needs.

Get you used to the "vibe" of the TEE questions.

Give you a "baseline" score so you can see your progress.

Checking Your Gauges
Once you've finished the assessment, use this scale to see where you sit. It'll help you decide how much time to spend on the tutorials before moving on to the full practice tests.

The goal here is to give you a baseline score. Once you finish, look at the table below to see how you stack up and what your next move should be.

Scoring Guide: Where Do You Stand?

Score Range	What it Means	Your Next Step
80% - 100%	You've got a sharp eye for detail.	Focus on your weaker subjects; just do a light review here.
60% - 79%	You're on the right track, but missing the finer points.	Go through the tutorials again and practice active reading.
Below 60%	This area is going to be a struggle on exam day.	Dig deep into the tutorials and consider extra reading exercises.

Self-Assessment Answer Sheet

	A	B	C	D	E			A	B	C	D	E
1	○	○	○	○	○		21	○	○	○	○	○
2	○	○	○	○	○		22	○	○	○	○	○
3	○	○	○	○	○		23	○	○	○	○	○
4	○	○	○	○	○		24	○	○	○	○	○
5	○	○	○	○	○		25	○	○	○	○	○
6	○	○	○	○	○							
7	○	○	○	○	○							
8	○	○	○	○	○							
9	○	○	○	○	○							
10	○	○	○	○	○							
11	○	○	○	○	○							
12	○	○	○	○	○							
13	○	○	○	○	○							
14	○	○	○	○	○							
15	○	○	○	○	○							
16	○	○	○	○	○							
17	○	○	○	○	○							
18	○	○	○	○	○							
19	○	○	○	○	○							
20	○	○	○	○	○							

Vocabulary & Context Clues and Grammar Practice

1. The journeyman warned the apprentice that the old iron pipe was prone to corrosion if left in the damp crawlspace. In this sentence, corrosion most likely means:

    a. Turning a different colour
    b. Bending under pressure
    c. Damage caused by chemical reaction or rust
    d. Becoming magnetic

2. Before starting the demolition, the site supervisor had to verify that the power was completely disconnected. To verify means to:

    a. Hope for the best
    b. Prove or check that something is true
    c. Change the direction of
    d. Repair a broken part

3. The safety manual states that all workers must wear high-visibility vests so they are conspicuous to heavy equipment operators. Conspicuous means:

    a. Easily seen or noticed
    b. Protected from the rain
    c. Trained in safety protocols
    d. Working in a restricted area

4. Because the workspace was so cramped, the plumber had to find a more compact set of wrenches to reach the bolts behind the tank. Compact means:

    a. Expensive and high-quality
    b. Heavy and durable
    c. Small and space-saving
    d. Painted a bright colour

5. While the initial estimate for the renovation was $5,000, the final cost was much higher due to several unforeseen structural issues found behind the walls. Unforeseen most nearly means:

    a. Planned in advance
    b. Not expected or predicted
    c. Extremely expensive
    d. Related to the foundation

6. The welder noticed a minute crack in the hull of the trailer that was almost impossible to see without a magnifying glass. In this context, minute (pronounced my-noot) means:

    a. A measurement of time
    b. Very small or insignificant in size
    c. Roughly textured
    d. Glowing brightly

7. To ensure the concrete sets properly, it is imperative that no one walks on the surface for at least twenty-four hours. Imperative means:

    a. Suggested but not required
    b. Extremely important or necessary
    c. Done at a slow pace
    d. Likely to happen

8. The technician had to calibrate the digital scale every morning to ensure the measurements of the chemical additives were perfectly accurate. To calibrate means to:

    a. Clean thoroughly with soap
    b. Record the weight in a logbook
    c. Adjust an instrument for accuracy
    d. Replace old batteries

9. After the heavy rainstorm, the foreman noted that the soil at the excavation site was saturated, making it unsafe to bring in the heavy crane. Saturated means:

    a. Completely soaked with liquid
    b. Very dry and dusty
    c. Frozen solid
    d. Slanted at an angle

10. The apprentice was told to be diligent when checking the torque on the wheel lugs, as a single loose bolt could lead to a major accident on the highway. Diligent means:

    a. Fast and efficient
    b. Showing steady and careful effort
    c. Working without supervision
    d. Using the newest tools available

11. The job site supervisor noted that the blueprint was extremely precise. Which of the following is a synonym for precise?

    a. Accurate
    b. Large
    c. Colourful
    d. Technical

12. The safety officer warned that the old floorboards were unstable. Which of the following is an antonym for unstable?

    a. Precarious
    b. Secure
    c. Rotting
    d. Temporary

13. When working with heavy machinery, it is vital to keep the workspace tidy. Which word has the same meaning as tidy?

    a. Spacious
    b. Orderly
    c. Bright
    d. Ventilated

14. The apprentice was told that the task was mandatory for all first-year students. What is the opposite of mandatory?

    a. Required
    b. Important
    c. Optional
    d. Difficult

15. During the inspection, the electrician found that the wiring was obsolete and needed to be replaced to meet current BC building codes. Which word is a synonym for obsolete?

    a. Dangerous
    b. Outdated
    c. Complex
    d. Expensive

16. The project manager explained that the timeline for the renovation was flexible, provided the plumbing was finished by Friday. What is an antonym for flexible in this scenario?

    a. Rigid
    b. Extended
    c. Realistic
    d. Reliable

17. The new hydraulic lift is much more efficient than the manual model used last year. In this context, what is a synonym for efficient?

    a. Costly
    b. Productive
    c. Modern
    d. Heavy

18. After the team lead provided the instructions, the worker remained hesitant to start the high-voltage testing. What is an antonym for hesitant?

    a. Reluctant
    b. Cautious
    c. Confident
    d. Qualified

19. To prevent injury, it is important to ensure that the lighting in the stairwell is adequate. What is a synonym for adequate?

    a. Excessive
    b. Sufficient
    c. Permanent
    d. Natural

20. The plumber noticed that the water pressure was fluctuating throughout the morning. What is the opposite of fluctuating?

    a. Increasing
    b. Changing
    c. Constant
    d. Dropping

Answer Key & Analysis

1. C (Rust/chemical damage).
Common Trap: Choice A While rust often changes the colour of metal, the actual word "corrosion" refers to the deterioration of the material itself.

2. B (To check/prove).

3. A (Easily seen).

4. C (Space-saving).

5. B (Not predicted). Common Trap: c. Structural issues are expensive, but "unforeseen" specifically describes the fact that they weren't seen ahead of time.

6. B (Very small). Common Trap: a. In a trade context, a "minute" crack refers to size, not the 60 seconds on a clock.

7. B (Necessary).

8. C (Adjust for accuracy).

9. A (Soaked).

10. B (Careful effort).

11. A
Precise means exact and accurate.

Option D is incorrect because something can be technical without being precise.

12. B
Unstable means wobbly or not firm; secure is the opposite.

Option D is a common trap; temporary relates to time, not physical stability.

13. B

Tidy and orderly both refer to things being in their proper place.

14. C

Mandatory means required; optional means you have a choice.

15. B

Obsolete means no longer produced or used; outdated.

Option A is a common trap; while obsolete wiring is often dangerous, the word itself just means old/outdated.

16. A

Flexible means able to change; rigid means fixed or unable to bend/change.

17. B

Efficient refers to achieving maximum productivity with minimum wasted effort.

18. C

Hesitant implies doubt; confident implies certainty in action.

19. B

Adequate means "good enough" or sufficient for the requirement.

20. C

Fluctuating means rising and falling irregularly; constant means staying the same.

English Grammar and Punctuation Tutorials

Capitalization: Making it Look Professional

Think of capitalization like a "High-Vis" vest for your words—it helps the important stuff stand out.

Starting the Sentence

We all know the first word gets a capital. But what happens after a colon (:) or a semicolon (;)?

- **The Colon Rule:** If you're writing a full sentence after a colon, capitalize it.
    - *Example:* The site is shut down: The crane operator didn't show up.
- **The List Rule:** If it's just a word or a list, keep it lowercase.
    - *Example:* We need three things: cedar, galvanized nails, and a level.
- **The Semicolon Rule:** Never capitalize the word after a semicolon unless it's a name. It's just a "strong comma."
    - *Example:* The plumbing is finished; the drywalling starts tomorrow.

Proper Nouns (Specific Names)

Capitalize the names of specific people, places, and brands.

- **Tools & Brands:** "The drill" (lowercase), but "the DeWalt drill" (capitalized).
- **Job Sites:** "The site" (lowercase), but "the Johnson Street Bridge Project" (capitalized).
- **Family & Titles:** Capitalize titles only when they replace a name.

- o *Right:* "I asked the Foreman for a raise."
- o *Right:* "Hey Mom, can you drop off my lunch?"
- o *Wrong:* "My mom is coming to the site."

Directions vs. Regions
This is a common trap in BC.

- **Direction (Lowercase):** "Drive north on the Malahat for twenty minutes."
- **Region (Capitalized):** "Most of our contracts are in the North." (Referring to Northern BC).

Punctuation: The Toolbelt of Writing

Colons (:) and Semicolons (;)

- **The Colon:** Use it to introduce a list or a "big reveal."
  - o *Example:* Don't forget the safety gear: boots, vest, and glasses.
- **The Semicolon:** Use it to join two related thoughts without using a word like "and" or "but."
  - o *Example:* The concrete is pouring; stay clear of the truck.

Hyphens (-) vs. Dashes (—)

- **Hyphens:** Use these to "weld" two words together into one idea.
  - o *Example:* A **well-maintained** truck; a **heavy-duty** winch.
- **Dashes:** Use a long dash to add a "by the way" thought at the end of a sentence.
  - o *Example:* The client was happy with the Reno—everyone got a bonus.

Apostrophes (')

These show ownership or missing letters.

- **Ownership:** "The **carpenter's** hammer" (one person) or "the **carpenters'** breakroom" (the whole crew).
- **The "S" Debate:** If a name ends in S (like Jones), both *Jones'* and *Jones's* are okay. Just pick one and stick to it so your invoices look consistent.

Commas: The "Breath" Marks

Commas keep your sentences from running off the road.

The "Oxford" Comma
In the trades, we prefer the "Oxford Comma" because it prevents accidents.
- *Confusing:* "I'd like to thank my parents, the Premier and God." (Makes it sound like your parents are the Premier and God).
- *Clear:* "I'd like to thank my parents, the Premier, and God." (Three separate groups).

Joining Thoughts
If you have two full thoughts joined by "and," "but," or "so," put a comma before the joiner.
- *Example:* The roof is leaking, and the owner is losing his mind.

Quotation Marks: Saying it Right

- **Punctuation stays inside:** In Canada, we keep the periods and commas inside the "bunny ears."
    - *Example:* Brian said, "Double-check the measurements."

- **Titles:** Use quotes for small things like a "Safety Memo" or a "Change Order." Use italics for big things like the *National Building Code*.

TEST 1: THE FOUNDATION BUILDER

A Note Before You Dive In

I'll be straight with you: these aren't the exact questions you'll see on the TEE. If anyone tells you they have the "real" questions, they're pulling your leg. The exam changes all the time to keep things fair.

However, we've spent years in the classroom and at the desk triple-checking these subject areas. While the wording might be a little different on the big day, the concepts are identical. If you can wrap your head around the questions below, you're going to do just fine on the TEE.

How to get the most out of this:

> **Make it "Real":** Find a quiet spot, put your phone away, and treat this like the actual exam.
>
> **Take Your Time:** Read every instruction and every question twice. Most mistakes happen from rushing, not from a lack of knowledge.

Use the Bubble Sheets: We've included them for a reason! Get used to the mechanics of the test now so it's second nature later.

Check the "Why": Once you're done, don't just look at what you got right or wrong. Read our explanations in the Answer Key. That's where the real learning happens.

One last bit of advice: Don't burn yourself out. Tackle one practice test today, then step away. Give your brain two or three days to chew on what you've learned before you try the next set. We're aiming for steady progress, not a midnight cram session.

Mathematics

	A	B	C	D	E		A	B	C	D	E
1	○	○	○	○	○	21	○	○	○	○	○
2	○	○	○	○	○	22	○	○	○	○	○
3	○	○	○	○	○	23	○	○	○	○	○
4	○	○	○	○	○	24	○	○	○	○	○
5	○	○	○	○	○	25	○	○	○	○	○
6	○	○	○	○	○						
7	○	○	○	○	○						
8	○	○	○	○	○						
9	○	○	○	○	○						
10	○	○	○	○	○						
11	○	○	○	○	○						
12	○	○	○	○	○						
13	○	○	○	○	○						
14	○	○	○	○	○						
15	○	○	○	○	○						
16	○	○	○	○	○						
17	○	○	○	○	○						
18	○	○	○	○	○						
19	○	○	○	○	○						
20	○	○	○	○	○						

Science

	A	B	C	D	E		A	B	C	D	E
1	○	○	○	○	○	21	○	○	○	○	○
2	○	○	○	○	○	22	○	○	○	○	○
3	○	○	○	○	○	23	○	○	○	○	○
4	○	○	○	○	○	24	○	○	○	○	○
5	○	○	○	○	○	25	○	○	○	○	○
6	○	○	○	○	○	26	○	○	○	○	○
7	○	○	○	○	○	27	○	○	○	○	○
8	○	○	○	○	○	28	○	○	○	○	○
9	○	○	○	○	○	29	○	○	○	○	○
10	○	○	○	○	○	30	○	○	○	○	○
11	○	○	○	○	○						
12	○	○	○	○	○						
13	○	○	○	○	○						
14	○	○	○	○	○						
15	○	○	○	○	○						
16	○	○	○	○	○						
17	○	○	○	○	○						
18	○	○	○	○	○						
19	○	○	○	○	○						
20	○	○	○	○	○						

Interpreting Specs, Codes & Manuals

	A	B	C	D	E			A	B	C	D	E
1	○	○	○	○	○		21	○	○	○	○	○
2	○	○	○	○	○		22	○	○	○	○	○
3	○	○	○	○	○		23	○	○	○	○	○
4	○	○	○	○	○		24	○	○	○	○	○
5	○	○	○	○	○		25	○	○	○	○	○
6	○	○	○	○	○							
7	○	○	○	○	○							
8	○	○	○	○	○							
9	○	○	○	○	○							
10	○	○	○	○	○							
11	○	○	○	○	○							
12	○	○	○	○	○							
13	○	○	○	○	○							
14	○	○	○	○	○							
15	○	○	○	○	○							
16	○	○	○	○	○							
17	○	○	○	○	○							
18	○	○	○	○	○							
19	○	○	○	○	○							
20	○	○	○	○	○							

Communication - English

	A	B	C	D
1	○	○	○	○
2	○	○	○	○
3	○	○	○	○
4	○	○	○	○
5	○	○	○	○
6	○	○	○	○
7	○	○	○	○
8	○	○	○	○
9	○	○	○	○
10	○	○	○	○
11	○	○	○	○
12	○	○	○	○
13	○	○	○	○
14	○	○	○	○
15	○	○	○	○
16	○	○	○	○
17	○	○	○	○
18	○	○	○	○
19	○	○	○	○
20	○	○	○	○

Mathematics

1. What is 1/3 of 3/4?

    a. 1/4
    b. 1/3
    c. 2/3
    d. 3/4

2. What fraction of $75 is $1500?

    a. 1/14
    b. 3/5
    c. 7/10
    d. 1/20

3. 3.14 + 2.73 + 23.7 =

    a. 28.57
    b. 30.57
    c. 29.56
    d. 29.57

4. A woman spent 15% of her income on an item and ends with $120. What percentage of her income is left?

    a. 12%
    b. 85%
    c. 75%
    d. 95%

5. Express 0.27 + 0.33 as a fraction.

    a. 3/6
    b. 4/7
    c. 3/5
    d. 2/7

6. What is (3.13 + 7.87) X 5?

    a. 65
    b. 50
    c. 45
    d. 55

7. Reduce 2/4 X 3/4 to lowest terms.

    a. 6/12
    b. 3/8
    c. 6/16
    d. 3/4

8. 2/3 − 2/5 =

    a. 4/10
    b. 1/15
    c. 3/7
    d. 4/15

9. 2/7 + 2/3 =

    a. 12/23
    b. 5/10
    c. 20/21
    d. 6/21

10. 2/3 of 60 + 1/5 of 75 =

    a. 45
    b. 55
    c. 15
    d. 50

11. 8 is what percent of 40?

    a. 10%
    b. 15%
    c. 20%
    d. 25%

12. 9 is what percent of 36?

    a. 10%
    b. 15%
    c. 20%
    d. 25%

13. Three tenths of 90 equals:

    a. 18
    b. 45
    c. 27
    d. 36

14. .4% of 36 is

    a. 1.44
    b. .144
    c. 14.4
    d. 144

15. If a welder earns $32.00 per hour and receives a 4% cost-of-living increase, what is their new hourly rate?

    a. $33.28
    b. $32.40
    c. $33.00
    d. $36.00

16. Convert 0.75 into a percentage.

    a. 7.5%
    b. 0.75%
    c. 75%
    d. 750%

17. A blueprint uses a scale of 1:50. If a wall measures 12 cm on the blueprint, what is the actual length of the wall in metres?

    a. 0.6 metres
    b. 6.0 metres
    c. 60 metres
    d. 600 metres

18. A pipe fitting is discounted by 15%. If the original price was $120.00, what is the new sale price?

    a. $102.00
    b. $105.00
    c. $18.00
    d. $115.00

19. A contractor needs to fence a rectangular yard that is 15 metres long and 10 metres wide. If fence posts must be placed every 2.5 metres (including the corners), how many posts are needed?

    a. 10
    b. 20
    c. 25
    d. 30

20. What is the perimeter of a square with sides measuring 8 cm?

    a. 16 cm
    b. 32 cm
    c. 64 cm
    d. 24 cm

21. What is the perimeter of a square with sides measuring 8 cm?

    a. 16 cm
    b. 32 cm
    c. 64 cm
    d. 24 cm

22. A container holds 4.5 litres of cleaning fluid. If a worker uses 750 ml, how much fluid remains in the container?

    a. 3.75 litres
    b. 4.25 litres
    c. 3.25 litres
    d. 3.5 litres

23. Add the following fractions: 1/4 + 3/8.

    a. 4/12
    b. 5/8
    c. 1/2
    d. 7/8

24. Divide 144 by 12.

    a. 10
    b. 12
    c. 14
    d. 11

25. A carpenter is building a staircase. The total rise is 210 cm. If each individual riser must be 17.5 cm high, how many steps are needed?

    a. 10
    b. 11
    c. 12
    d. 14

Science

1. Which of the following is a physical property of matter rather than a chemical property?

    a. Reactivity with water
    b. Flammability
    c. Boiling point
    d. Susceptibility to corrosion

2. A pneumatic tool is connected to an air compressor. If the pressure gauge reads 90 PSI (Pounds per Square Inch), what does this pressure actually represent?

    a. The speed at which the air is moving through the hose.
    b. The force exerted by the air on every square inch of the container walls.
    c. The total volume of air stored in the tank.
    d. The temperature of the air inside the tool.

3. A technician is using a Class 2 lever (like a wheelbarrow) to move a heavy load. If the technician moves the load further away from their hands and closer to the wheel (the fulcrum), what is the result?

    a. It becomes harder to lift because the effort arm is shorter.
    b. It becomes easier to lift because the resistance arm is shorter.
    c. The mechanical advantage decreases.
    d. The wheelbarrow becomes more prone to tipping backward.

4. A soldering iron works by passing electricity through a material that resists the flow of current. This resistance generates:

    a. Static electricity
    b. Magnetic fields
    c. Heat
    d. Voltage

5. In a gear train, if Gear A (20 teeth) is the driver and Gear B (10 teeth) is the driven gear, what is the gear ratio?

    a. 1:2
    b. 2:1
    c. 1:1
    d. 20:1

6. A hydraulic jack is used to lift a vehicle. The small piston is pushed down, which moves the large piston up. Why does the large piston move with more force than was applied to the small one?

    a. The large piston has more surface area for the pressure to act upon.
    b. The fluid becomes denser as it moves to the large piston.
    c. Friction is eliminated in hydraulic systems.
    d. The large piston moves a greater distance than the small one.

7. You are working outside in a BC winter where the temperature is -10 degrees Celsius. You need to ensure a piece of machinery doesn't freeze. What is the approximate temperature in Fahrenheit?

    a. -10 F
    b. 32 F
    c. 14 F
    d. 0 F

8. Which state of matter has a definite volume but no definite shape, taking the shape of its container?

   a. Solid
   b. Liquid
   c. Gas
   d. Plasma

9. You notice a piece of copper pipe and a piece of plastic pipe lying in the sun. The copper pipe feels much hotter to the touch than the plastic one. This is because copper has a higher:

   a. Specific heat capacity
   b. Thermal conductivity
   c. Electrical resistance
   d. Density

10. If you increase the Voltage in a circuit but keep the Resistance the same, what happens to the Amperage?

    a. The Amperage increases.
    b. The Amperage decreases.
    c. The Amperage stays the same.
    d. The circuit becomes a short circuit.

11. The term "Mechanical Advantage" refers to:

    a. The speed at which a machine operates.
    b. The ratio of output force to input force in a machine.
    c. The weight of the machine itself.
    d. The time it takes to set up a tool.

12. A worker is pouring a thick oil into an engine on a cold morning. The oil flows very slowly. This resistance to flow is known as:

    a. Density
    b. Viscosity
    c. Buoyancy
    d. Flashpoint

13. A shop fan is plugged into an outlet and is running. If the motor begins to seize up due to a bad bearing, the resistance in the motor increases. What is the most likely electrical result?

    a. The motor will draw fewer Amps and run cooler.
    b. The voltage from the outlet will increase to compensate.
    c. The motor will draw more Amps, generate excess heat, and potentially blow a fuse.
    d. The fan will spin faster to try and overcome the friction.

14. You are using a block and tackle (pulley system) with 4 ropes supporting the load. To lift a 400 lb engine, how much force must you apply?

    a. 400 lbs
    b. 100 lbs
    c. 200 lbs
    d. 50 lbs

15. What does the "W" in WHMIS stand for?

    a. Worker
    b. Workplace
    c. Warning
    d. Waste

16. A pressure cooker or a sealed boiler shows that as you increase the pressure on a liquid, its boiling point:

    a. Decreases
    b. Stays the same
    c. Increases
    d. Disappears

17. In a shop, you have a heavy steel plate leaning against a wall. If the plate falls flat onto the floor, its potential energy is converted into:

    a. Kinetic energy and sound/heat.
    b. Chemical energy.
    c. Electrical energy.
    d. Static electricity.

18. Which of the following is the best conductor of electricity?

    a. Rubber
    b. Glass
    c. Copper
    d. Wood

19. A technician is checking a car battery. The battery is rated at 12 Volts. If the technician measures the resistance of the starter motor as 0.05 Ohms, how many Amps will the battery need to provide to start the car?

    a. 240 Amps
    b. 0.6 Amps
    c. 12.05 Amps
    d. 60 Amps

20. When using a wedge (like an axe) to split wood, the wedge is technically a type of:

    a. Lever
    b. Pulley
    c. Inclined plane
    d. Gear

21. Which of the following illustrates the principal of the lever?

    a. The greater the distance over which the force is applied, the greater the force required (to lift the load).

    b. The greater the distance over which the force is applied, the smaller the force required (to lift the load).

    c. The smaller the distance over which the force is applied, the smaller the force required (to lift the load).

    d. None of the above

22. Consider two gears on separate shafts that mesh. The input gear has 30 teeth and turns at 100 rpm. If the output gear has 40 teeth, how fast is the output gear turning?

    a. 300 rpm
    b. 250 rpm
    c. 75 rpm
    d. 100 rpm

23. Consider two gears on separate shafts that mesh. The input gear has 100 teeth and turns at 50 rpm. If the output gear has 20 teeth, how fast is the output gear turning?

    a. 300 rpm
    b. 250 rpm
    c. 200 rpm
    d. 100 rpm

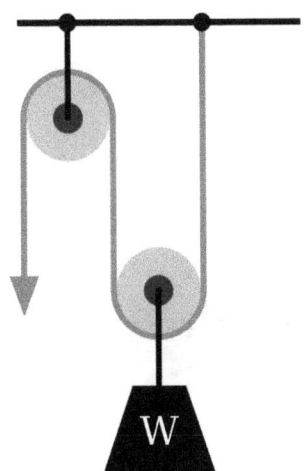

24. Consider the pulley arrangement above. If the weight is 100 pounds, how much force is required to lift it?

    a. 20 pounds
    b. 33 pounds
    c. 50 pounds
    d. 75 pounds

25. Tension of 40 kg. is applied to two springs in parallel, which expands the springs 8 inches. If the same force is applied to springs in series, how far will the springs expand?

    a. 2 inches
    b. 4 inches
    c. 8 inches
    d. 16 inches

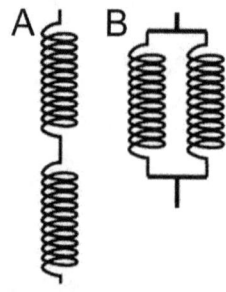

26. Consider the diagram above and select the correct labels from the options below.

    a. A - series, B - parallel

    b. A - parallel, B - series

    c. Series and parallel do not apply to springs

    d. None of the above

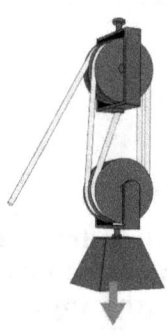

27. Consider the pulley arrangement above. If the weight is 200 pounds, how much force must be exerted downward on the rope?

    a. 200 pounds
    b. 100 pounds
    c. 50 pounds
    d. 25 pounds

28. Up-and-down or back-and-forth motion is called:

    a. Rotary motion
    b. Reciprocating motion
    c. Agitation motion
    d. Harmonic motion

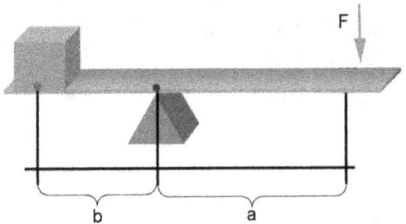

39. Consider the illustration above and the corresponding data:

Weight = W = 80 pounds
Distance from fulcrum to Weight = b = 10 feet
Distance from fulcrum to point where force is applied = a = 20 feet
How much force (F) must be applied to lift the weight?

    a. 80
    b. 40
    c. 20
    d. 10

30. The output torque of a 2 gear train is 1,000 newton-meters, and the gear ratio is 2:1. What is the input force?

   a. 200
   b. 400
   c. 500
   d. 1000

Interpreting Specs, Codes & Manuals

Directions: The following questions are based on several reading passages. Each passage is followed by a series of questions. Read each passage carefully, and then answer the questions based on it. You may reread the passage as often as you wish. When you have finished answering the questions based on one passage, go right onto the next passage. Choose the best answer based on the information given and implied.

General Shop Safety & PPE Policy

"All personnel entering the active fabrication zone must wear Grade 1 protective footwear (green triangle patch). When operating fixed machinery, such as a drill press or bench grinder, eye protection must be worn in addition to a full-face shield if the material being worked produces flying chips or sparks. Hearing protection is mandatory only when noise levels exceed 85 decibels (dB) for a duration of more than 15 minutes. Loose-fitting clothing and jewelry must be removed or secured before engaging any rotating equipment."

1. According to the policy, what symbol must be visible on the protective footwear of workers in the fabrication zone?

    a. A yellow square
    b. A green triangle
    c. A red circle
    d. A blue hexagon

2. A worker is using a bench grinder to sharpen a chisel, which is producing significant sparks. According to the manual, what is the required eye/face protection?

    a. Safety glasses only
    b. A full-face shield only
    c. Safety glasses and a full-face shield
    d. No protection is required for short tasks

3. A technician is working near a generator that produces 90 dB of noise. They will be in the area for a total of 10 minutes to perform a quick inspection. Is hearing protection mandatory?

    a. Yes, because the noise is over 85 dB
    b. Yes, because all generators require hearing protection
    c. No, because the duration is less than 15 minutes
    d. No, because 90 dB is considered a safe level

4. A new apprentice arrives at the fabrication zone wearing Grade 1 boots and safety glasses. They are wearing a loose-fitting hoodie and a wedding ring. They are assigned to help a journeyman operate a lathe (rotating equipment). Based on the manual, what must occur before they start?

    a. They only need to put on a face shield

    b. They must remove the hoodie and the ring

    c. They can start as long as they stay 2 meters away

    d. They must change their boots to Grade 2

Torque Specifications & Fasteners

"When assembling the Model-X manifold, bolts must be tightened in a 'star pattern' to ensure even pressure. Initial torque should be set to 15 foot-pounds (ft-lbs). Once all bolts are seated, a final pass must be made to reach a specification of 35 ft-lbs. Do not use pneumatic impact wrenches for the final pass, as this can lead to over-tightening and thread stripping. Always inspect threads for debris or 'burrs' before insertion."

5. What is the final torque specification for the Model-X manifold bolts?

    a. 15 ft-lbs

    b. 25 ft-lbs

    c. 35 ft-lbs

    d. 50 ft-lbs

6. Why does the manual specifically forbid the use of pneumatic impact wrenches for the final torque pass?

    a. They are too slow for assembly line work

    b. They may cause over-tightening or damage to threads

    c. They do not work with a star pattern

    d. They require too much compressed air

7. A mechanic finds a small metal "burr" (a sharp imperfection) on the threads of a bolt before putting it into the manifold. Based on the instructions, what should the mechanic do?

    a. Ignore it and use a high-torque wrench to force it in
    b. Use a pneumatic wrench to clear the debris
    c. Address the burr or replace the bolt before insertion
    d. Use extra lubricant to slide the bolt past the burr

8. You are supervising an apprentice who is tightening the manifold bolts. They tighten the first bolt to 35 ft-lbs, then move to the bolt directly next to it and tighten it to 35 ft-lbs. Which two instructions from the manual are they violating?

    a. Initial torque setting and the star pattern
    b. Tool selection and thread inspection
    c. Lubrication requirements and final torque
    d. Grade of bolt and sequence

Circuit Breaker Maintenance Log

"Note: Before resetting any tripped breaker in the Main Distribution Frame (MDF), the technician must first identify the cause of the fault. If a breaker trips a second time immediately after being reset, do not attempt a third reset. Tag the breaker 'Out of Service' and notify the Lead Electrician. Maintenance logs must be updated with the time, date, and breaker ID number within 30 minutes of the incident."

9. What information must be recorded in the maintenance log after a breaker incident?

    a. Only the technician's name
    b. Time, date, and breaker ID number
    c. The cost of the replacement parts
    d. The weather conditions at the time

10. A technician resets a breaker that tripped. Two minutes later, the breaker trips again. According to the manual, what is the technician's next step?

    a. Try resetting it one more time

    b. Hold the breaker in the 'On' position manually

    c. Tag it 'Out of Service' and notify the Lead Electrician

    d. Replace the breaker immediately without notification

11. A breaker trips at 10:00 AM. The technician identifies the fault (a dusty motor) and clears it. By what time must the maintenance log be updated?

    a. 10:15 AM

    b. 10:30 AM

    c. 11:00 AM

    d. By the end of the shift

12. A breaker trips. The technician resets it, and it stays on. They decide to wait until the end of the day to fill out the maintenance log because they have several other tasks to complete. Which part of the protocol is being violated?

    a. The requirement to identify the cause of the fault

    b. The requirement to tag the breaker "Out of Service"

    c. The 30-minute timeframe for logging the incident

    d. The requirement to notify the Lead Electrician

Mixing and Curing Concrete

"For standard footings, use a 1:2:4 ratio (1 part cement, 2 parts sand, 4 parts gravel). Water should be added slowly until a 'slump' of 3 to 4 inches is achieved. If the ambient temperature is below 5°C, chemical accelerators may be used to speed up the curing process. Once poured, concrete must be kept moist for at least 7 days to reach maximum design strength."

13. In the 1:2:4 mixing ratio, what material represents the '4 parts'?

    a. Cement
    b. Sand
    c. Water
    d. Gravel

Question 14 The temperature at a job site in Prince George is currently 2°C. According to the specs, what adjustment can be made? a. Add more gravel to the mix b. Use chemical accelerators c. Use less water to prevent freezing d. Reduce the curing time to 3 days

15. A worker is testing the "slump" of a fresh batch of concrete and finds it is only 1 inch (meaning it is very stiff/dry). What is the most likely corrective action based on the passage?

    a. Add more gravel
    b. Remove some sand
    c. Slowly add more water
    d. Pour it immediately before it hardens

16. A contractor pours a footing on Monday. On Friday, they stop spraying the concrete with water, claiming it "looks dry enough." Why is this a violation of the specifications?

    a. Concrete needs to stay dry to cure properly
    b. It must be kept moist for 7 days to reach full strength
    c. Footings must be cured for at least 14 days
    d. Chemical accelerators were not used

Ladder Safety and Load Limits

"Type I Heavy Duty ladders have a load capacity of 250 lbs. This weight includes the user, their clothing, and all tools or materials carried onto the ladder. When setting up an extension ladder, use the 4-to-1 rule: for every 4 feet of height, the base should be 1 foot away from the wall. Always maintain three points of contact while climbing."

17. What is the maximum load capacity for a Type I Heavy Duty ladder?

    a. 200 lbs

    b. 250 lbs

    c. 300 lbs

    d. 350 lbs

18. A technician weighs 210 lbs. They are wearing a tool belt that weighs 25 lbs and are carrying a piece of equipment that weighs 20 lbs. Are they within the load limit for a Type I ladder?

    a. Yes, they are exactly at 250 lbs

    b. Yes, they are at 210 lbs because equipment doesn't count

    c. No, their total weight is 255 lbs

    d. No, Type I ladders are only for tools, not people

19. If a worker needs to reach a height of 12 feet on a wall using an extension ladder, how far should the base of the ladder be from the wall?

    a. 1 foot

    b. 2 feet

    c. 3 feet

    d. 4 feet

20. A worker is climbing a ladder while carrying a heavy toolbox in one hand and a drill in the other. They are using their feet to climb but have no hands free to grip the rungs. Which safety rule are they violating?

    a. The 4-to-1 rule

    b. The 250 lbs load limit

    c. The three points of contact rule

    d. The Grade 1 footwear rule

Storage of Compressed Gas Cylinders

"Oxygen and fuel-gas cylinders (such as acetylene) must be stored at least 20 feet (6 meters) apart unless separated by a non-combustible wall at least 5 feet high with a fire-resistance rating of 30 minutes. All cylinders must be stored upright and secured with chains to prevent tipping. Valve protection caps must be in place whenever cylinders are not in use or are being moved."

21. How should cylinders be stored to prevent tipping?

    a. Lying flat on the ground

    b. Stacked on top of each other

    c. Upright and secured with chains

    d. Leaning against a wall

22. A shop has oxygen and acetylene cylinders stored 10 feet apart. There is no wall between them. Does this meet the safety standard?

    a. Yes, 10 feet is sufficient for small shops

    b. Yes, as long as the caps are on

    c. No, they must be at least 20 feet apart without a barrier

    d. No, they can never be stored in the same room

23. When should valve protection caps be on the cylinders?

    a. Only when the cylinder is empty

    b. Only during long-term storage

    c. Whenever the cylinder is not in use or is being moved

    d. Only when requested by a supervisor

24. A worker builds a 4-foot tall wooden wall to separate oxygen and fuel cylinders stored 5 feet apart. Why does this NOT meet the requirement described in the passage?

    a. The wall is too short and the material is combustible

    b. The wall must be made of reinforced steel

    c. Cylinders must be 20 feet apart regardless of a wall

    d. Chains are not required if a wall is present

25. What is the required fire-resistance rating for a wall used to separate gas cylinders?

    a. 15 minutes

    b. 30 minutes

    c. 60 minutes

    d. 2 hours

Communication - English

1. On a job site, what does the term "PPE" stand for?

    a. Professional Power Equipment
    b. Personal Protective Equipment
    c. Primary Pressure Engine
    d. Public Prevention Entry

2. A supervisor tells you that a specific tool is "stationary." This means the tool:

    a. Is currently out of order
    b. Is powered by a battery
    c. Is fixed in one place and not meant to be moved
    d. Is made of high-quality stainless steel

3. In the trades, what does the term "specs" (short for specifications) usually refer to?

    a. Safety glasses worn during grinding
    b. The cost estimate for a specific project
    c. The precise measurements and requirements for a job
    d. The specialized tools required for a task

4. If a piece of equipment is described as "defective," it is:

    a. Brand new and ready for use
    b. Imperfect or not functioning correctly
    c. Highly efficient and fast
    d. Required to be used with a partner

5. During a renovation, the lead carpenter tells you that the wall is "plumb." This means:

    a. The wall is perfectly horizontal
    b. The wall is perfectly vertical (straight up and down)
    c. The wall is ready for plumbing pipes to be installed
    d. The wall is load-bearing and cannot be moved

6. A mechanic asks you to check the "clearance" between two moving parts. What is the mechanic asking you to measure?

    a. The total weight of the parts
    b. The speed at which the parts move
    c. The amount of space or gap between the parts
    d. The length of time the parts have been in use

7. You are told to ensure that a heavy load is "secured" before transport. This means you must:

   a. Check the weight of the load on a scale
   b. Make sure the load is fastened or tied down so it won't move
   c. Cover the load with a waterproof tarp
   d. Place the load in the center of the truck bed

8. If a supervisor mentions that a deadline is "imminent," you should understand that the deadline is:

   a. Likely to be cancelled
   b. Many weeks away
   c. About to happen very soon
   d. Flexible and open to negotiation

9. In a workshop, what is meant by the "capacity" of a storage tank?

   a. The physical weight of the empty tank
   b. The maximum amount the tank can hold
   c. The year the tank was manufactured
   d. The type of liquid currently inside the tank

10. A journeyman mentions that a surface needs to be "abraded" before the adhesive is applied. This means the surface should be:

    a. Cleaned with a chemical solvent
    b. Roughed up or worn down by friction (like sanding)
    c. Heated with a torch to remove moisture
    d. Coated in a thin layer of primer

11. Choose the word that correctly completes the following sentence: The supervisor asked the apprentices to leave _____ tools in the lockers before going to lunch.

    a. there
    b. their
    c. they're
    d. there's

12. A safety report needs to be filed. Which sentence uses correct capitalization and punctuation?

    a. The Inspector visited the Site on Tuesday, he noted three safety violations.
    b. the inspector visited the site on Tuesday; he noted three safety violations.
    c. The inspector visited the site on Tuesday; he noted three safety violations.
    d. The inspector visited the site on tuesday: he noted three safety violations.

13. Which of the following sentences regarding a work crew is grammatically correct?

    a. The crew of electricians is arriving at the job site at 07:00.
    b. The crew of electricians are arriving at the job site at 07:00.
    c. The crew of electricians were arriving at the job site at 07:00.
    d. The crew of electricians have arrived at the job site at 07:00.

14. Identify the error in the following site memo: "Neither the foreman nor the site workers was aware that the shipment of cedar had been delayed by the heavy snowfall in the interior."

    a. The word "Neither" should be "Either."
    b. The verb "was" should be "were."
    c. The word "cedar" should be capitalized.
    d. There should be a comma after "aware."

15. Which word correctly completes this sentence: The hydraulic lift has lost _____ pressure over the weekend.

    a. its
    b. it's
    c. its'
    d. it is

16. Select the sentence that avoids a run-on error.

a. Please check the oil level in the generator it has been running for twelve hours straight.
b. Please check the oil level in the generator, it has been running for twelve hours straight.
c. Please check the oil level in the generator; because it has been running for twelve hours straight.
d. Please check the oil level in the generator because it has been running for twelve hours straight.

17. Which sentence is punctuated correctly for a professional email?

a. We need to order more copper pipe, welding rods, and flux.
b. We need to order more; copper pipe, welding rods and flux.
c. We need to order more: copper pipe, welding rods, and flux.
d. We need to order more copper pipe welding rods and flux.

18. In the following sentence, choose the correct verb form: A list of all required safety equipment _____ posted on the bulletin board in the breakroom.

a. are
b. were
c. is
d. have been

19. Identify the sentence fragment:

a. Welding requires a steady hand.
b. Because the weather was too cold for the concrete to set.
c. The project was completed on time.
d. Stop the machine immediately.

20. Read the following sentence: "The lead carpenter, along with his two assistants, are finishing the cabinetry for the kitchen renovation in Oak Bay." What is the grammatical error?

    a. "Oak Bay" should not be capitalized.
    b. "are" should be "is."
    c. There should be no commas around "along with his two assistants."
    d. "kitchen" should be capitalized.

Answer Key and Analysis

Mathematics

1. A
1/3 X 3/4 = 3/12 = 1/4

2. D
75/1500 = 15/300 = 3/60 = 1/20

3. D
3.14 + 2.73 = 5.87 and 5.87 + 23.7 = 29.57

4. B
She spent 15% so, 100% - 15% = 85%

5. C
To convert a decimal to a fraction, take the places of decimal as your denominator, here, 2, so in 0.27, '7' is in the 100th place, so the fraction is 27/100 and 0.33 becomes 33/100.

Next estimate the answer quickly to eliminate obvious wrong choices. 27/100 is about 1/4 and 33/100 is 1/3. 1/3 is slightly larger than 1/4, and 1/4 + 1/4 is 1/2, so the answer will be slightly larger than 1/2.

Looking at the choices, Choice A can be eliminated since 3/6 = 1/2. Choice D, 2/7 is less than 1/2 and can be eliminated. so the answer is going to be Choice B or Choice C.
Do the calculation, 0.27 + 0.33 = 0.60 and 0.60 = 60/100 = 3/5, Choice C is correct.

6. D
3.13 + 7.87 = 11 and 11 X 5 = 55

7. B
2/4 X 3/4 = 6/16, and reduced to the lowest terms = 3/8

8. D
2/3-2/5 = 10-6 /15 = 4/15

9. C
2/7 + 2/3 = 6+14 /21 (21 is the common denominator) = 20/21

10. B
2/3 x 60 = 40 and 1.5 x 75 = 15, 40 + 15 = 55

11. C
This is an easy question, and shows how you can solve some questions without doing the calculations. The question is, 8 is what percent of 40. Take easy percentages for an approximate answer and see what you get.
10% is easy to calculate because you can drop the zero, or move the decimal point. 10% of 40 = 4, and 8 = 2 X 4, so, 8 must be 2 X 10% = 20%.

Here are the calculations which confirm the quick approximation.
8/40 = X/100 = 8 * 100 / 40X = 800/40 = X = 20

12. D
This is the same type of question which illustrates another method to solve quickly without doing the calculations. The question is, 9 is what percent of 36?

Ask, what is the relationship between 9 and 36? 9 X 4 = 36 so they are related by a factor of 4. If 9 is related to 36 by a factor of 4, then what is related to 100 (to get a percent) by a factor of 4?

To visualize:

9 X 4 = 36
Z X 4 = 100

So the answer is 25. 9 has the same relation to 36 as 25 has to 100.

Here are the calculations which confirm the quick approximation.
9/36 = X/100 = 9 * 100 / 36X = 900/36 = 25

13. C
3/10 * 90 = 3 * 90/10 = 27

14. B
.4% of 35 = 0.144

15. A
32 × 1.04 = 33.28

16. C
0.75 × 100 = 75%

17. B
12 × 50 = 600 cm = 6 metres

18. A
120 - 18 = 102

19. B
Perimeter is 50m. 50 / 2.5 = 20

20. B
8 × 4 = 32

21. B
8 × 4 = 32

22. A
4500ml - 750ml = 3750ml = 3.75L

23. B
2/8 + 3/8 = 5/8

24. B

25. C
210 / 17.5 = 12

Science

1. C
Boiling point can be observed without changing the identity of the substance.

2. B
Pressure is force per unit area.

3. B
Shortening the resistance arm (distance from load to fulcrum) makes the load easier to lift.

4. C
Resistance in a conductor generates heat (Joule heating).

5. B
Driver (20) / Driven (10) = 2. It turns twice as fast.

6. A
Pascal's Law states pressure is equal everywhere; force = pressure x area.

7. C
(-10 X 1.8) + 32 = -18 + 32 = 14. *Common Trap:* People often think -10C is 0F or -10F, but 32 is the freezing point.

8. B
Liquids have fixed volume but variable shape.

9. B
Metals conduct heat much faster than plastics.

10. A
V and I are directly proportional.

11. B
It's how much the machine "multiplies" your force.

12. B
Viscosity is "thickness" or resistance to flow.

13. C
When a motor struggles, it draws more current (Amps) to try to maintain speed, causing heat.

14. B
400 lbs / 4 supporting ropes = 100 lbs of effort.

15. B
Workplace Hazardous Materials Information System.

16. C
Higher pressure forces molecules to stay in liquid form longer.

17. A
Stored energy (potential) becomes movement (kinetic) and then dissipates as sound/heat on impact.

18. C
Copper has very low resistance.

19. A
12 / 0.05 = 240.

20. C
A wedge is two inclined planes joined back-to-back.

21. B
The greater the distance over which the force is applied, the smaller the force required (to lift the load).

22. C
Call the input gear G^1 and the output gear G^2. Call the speed of G^1, S^1 and the number of teeth T^1. Similarly for G^2, we have S^2 and T^2.
Given data:
$S^1 = 100$
$T^1 = 30$
$S^2 = $ unknown
$T^2 = 40$
We know that $S^1 \times T^1 = S^2 \times T^2$
So, $100 \times 30 = S^2 \times 40$
$S^2 = 3000/40 = 75$ rpm

23. B
Call the input gear G^1 and the output gear G^2. Call the speed of G^1, S^1 and the number of teeth T^1. Similarly for G^2, we have S^2 and T^2.
Given data
$S^1 - 50$
$T^1 = 100$
$S^2 = $ unknown

$T^2 = 20$
We know that $S^1 \times T^1 = S^2 \times T^2$

So, $50 \times 100 = S^2 \times 20$
$S^2 = 5000/20 = 250$ rpm

24. B
Notice the weight is attached to one end of the rope and to one pulley. The force required to lift a 100 pound weight with this arrangement is $100/3 = 33$.

25. A
If the springs in parallel expand 10 inches, then the springs in series will expand twice that amount, or 20 inches.

26. A
The correct labels are, A - series, B - parallel

27. C
50 pounds of force much be exerted downward on the rope to lift the 200 pound weight. Since there are 4 pulleys, each will take 1/4 of the load. $200/4 = 50$ pounds.

28. B
Up-and-down or back-and-forth motion is called reciprocal motion.

29. B
To solve for F, Weight X b (distance from fulcrum to weight) = Force X a (distance from fulcrum to point where force is applied)
$80 \times 10 = F \times 20$
$800/20 = F$
$F = 40$

30. C
If the output force is 1,000 newton-meters, and the gear ration is 2:1, the input force will be $1,000/2 = 500$.

Interpreting Specs, Codes & Manuals

1. B
The passage explicitly mentions the "green triangle patch" for Grade 1 footwear.

Choice A is incorrect (yellow square is for Grade 2).

Choices C and D are incorrect (not standard Canadian safety symbols for this context).

2. C
The text states that eye protection must be worn in addition to a full-face shield if material produces sparks.

Choice A is incorrect (ignores the face shield requirement).

Choice B is incorrect (ignores the eye protection requirement).

Common Trap: Choice B is a trap because workers often think a face shield replaces safety glasses, but the manual says "in addition to."

3. C
Hearing protection is only mandatory if levels exceed 85 dB for more than 15 minutes. The worker is only there for 10.

Choice A is incorrect (ignores the time duration).

Choice D is incorrect (90 dB is above the 85 dB threshold mentioned).

4. B
The manual requires loose clothing and jewelry to be "removed or secured" before engaging rotating equipment.

Choice A is incorrect (doesn't address the loose clothing/jewlry).

Choice D is incorrect (they already have Grade 1 boots).

5. C
The passage states: "final pass must be made to reach a specification of 35 ft-lbs."

Choice A is the initial torque.

6. B
The manual explicitly warns that these tools lead to "over-tightening and thread stripping."

Choice C is incorrect (you can use an impact wrench in any pattern, but it's not the reason for the ban here).

7. C
The manual says to "Always inspect threads... before insertion," implying that if a burr is found, it must be dealt with.

Choice A is incorrect (forcing it causes damage).

8. A
By tightening to 35 immediately (skipping the 15 ft-lbs initial pass) and moving to the adjacent bolt (skipping the star pattern), they violated two rules.
Choice B is incorrect (we don't know what tool they used).

9. B
Directly stated in the text: "time, date, and breaker ID number."

10. C
The manual says "If a breaker trips a second time... do not attempt a third reset. Tag the breaker 'Out of Service'..."

Common Trap: Choice a is a trap because in many homes people try a third time, but the manual strictly forbids it.

11. B
The log must be updated "within 30 minutes of the incident" (10:00 + 30 mins = 10:30).

12. C
The issue here is the timing. Waiting until the end of the day exceeds the 30-minute limit.

13. D
In the ratio 1:2:4 (Cement:Sand:Gravel), 4 represents gravel.

14. B
The text says "If the ambient temperature is below 5°C, chemical accelerators may be used."

Choices A and C are not mentioned as solutions in the text.

15. C
The manual says to add water slowly until a slump of 3-4 inches is reached. A 1-inch slump is too dry.

16. B
The manual states concrete must be kept moist for "at least 7 days." Monday to Friday is only 4-5 days.

17. B
Directly stated as 250 lbs.

18. C
210 (person) + 25 (tools) + 20 (equipment) = 255 lbs, which exceeds the 250 lbs limit.

Common Trap: Choice a is a trap if the student miscalculates or forgets to include the equipment weight.

19. C
Using the 4-to-1 rule: 12 feet / 4 = 3 feet.

20. C
To have three points of contact, you usually need two feet and one hand, or two hands and one foot. Having both hands full makes this impossible.

21. C
Directly stated in the text.

22. C
The rule is 20 feet apart unless separated by a wall. Since there is no wall, 10 feet is insufficient.

23. C
Directly stated: "whenever cylinders are not in use or are being moved."

24. A
The manual requires a wall at least 5 feet high (this was 4) and non-combustible (wood is combustible).

25. B
Directly stated in the text as 30 minutes.

> **Test Tip:** When a reading passage includes numbers (like "15 minutes," "30 minutes," or "20 feet"), the test creator is almost certainly going to ask a question about them. Always double-check if a scenario meets all the numerical requirements, not just one.

Communication - English

1. B
PPE is the standard acronym for equipment like hard hats, gloves, and boots.

2. C
Stationary comes from the root word for "standing" or "static."

3. C
"Specs" are the rules of the build. Common Trap: a. While safety glasses are "spectacles," in a trade context, "specs" almost always refers to the blueprint requirements.

4. B
A defect is a flaw.

5. B
Plumb is vertical; level is horizontal. This is a foundational trade term.

6. C
Clearance refers to the "clear" space between objects.

7. B
Securing involves preventing movement or theft.

8. C
Imminent means "right now" or "about to happen."

9. B
Capacity refers to volume or limit.

10. B
Abrading (like using an abrasive) creates "tooth" for paint or glue to stick to.

11. B
"Their" is the possessive pronoun for a group.

Choice A is "there" (location).

Choice C is "they're" (they are).

Choice D is "there's" (there is).

12. C
"The inspector" is a common noun and should not be capitalized. A semicolon is used to join two independent sentences.

Choice A is a comma splice.

Choice B fails to capitalize the first word.

Choice D fails to capitalize Tuesday.

13. A
"Crew" is a collective noun acting as a single unit, so it takes the singular verb "is."

Common Trap: Choice B is the trap; people often see "electricians" (plural) and choose "are," but the subject is "crew."

14. B
When using "neither/nor," the verb must agree with the subject closest to it. "Workers" is plural, so it should be "were."

Choice A is incorrect; "Neither" is correct here.

ChoiceC is incorrect; wood types are common nouns.

15. A
"Its" is the possessive form.

Choice B is "it is."

Choice C is not a real word.

16. D
This uses a conjunction ("because") to correctly join two clauses.

Choice A is a run-on.

Choice B is a comma splice.

17. A
Simple series punctuation with commas is correct.

Choice C is incorrect because you don't use a colon after "need."

18. C
The subject is "list" (singular), not "equipment."

Choice A and B are plural.

19. B
This is a dependent clause standing alone, making it a fragment.

20. B
The subject is "carpenter." Phrases like "along with" do not change the subject to plural.

Choice C is incorrect; those commas are necessary.

The "Ready for Game Day" Practice Session

You won't find these exact questions on the TEE—if we could do that, it'd be a pretty short study session! The truth is, nobody outside the exam room knows exactly what they'll ask, and the test changes every year. But don't let that worry you. We've designed these questions to cover the same ground and hit the same subject areas you're going to face. If you can handle what's on these pages, you're ready for the real thing.

To get the most out of this, try to "simulate" the exam. Find a quiet corner, turn off your phone, and give yourself the time to focus without any interruptions. Read every instruction and every question carefully—sometimes the smallest word makes the biggest difference.

A few tips for the best results:

Use the bubble sheets: It's good practice for the mechanical side of the test.

Check your work: Once you're done, head over to the Answer Key. Don't just look at the right answer; read our explanations to understand the "why" behind it.

Take a breather: Don't try to cram every practice test into one afternoon. Your brain needs time to soak in what you've learned. If you just finished Set 1, give it two or three days before you dive into this one.

Trades Entrance Exam

Mathematics

	A	B	C	D	E			A	B	C	D	E
1	○	○	○	○	○		21	○	○	○	○	○
2	○	○	○	○	○		22	○	○	○	○	○
3	○	○	○	○	○		23	○	○	○	○	○
4	○	○	○	○	○		24	○	○	○	○	○
5	○	○	○	○	○		25	○	○	○	○	○
6	○	○	○	○	○							
7	○	○	○	○	○							
8	○	○	○	○	○							
9	○	○	○	○	○							
10	○	○	○	○	○							
11	○	○	○	○	○							
12	○	○	○	○	○							
13	○	○	○	○	○							
14	○	○	○	○	○							
15	○	○	○	○	○							
16	○	○	○	○	○							
17	○	○	○	○	○							
18	○	○	○	○	○							
19	○	○	○	○	○							
20	○	○	○	○	○							

Science

	A	B	C	D	E		A	B	C	D	E
1	○	○	○	○	○	21	○	○	○	○	○
2	○	○	○	○	○	22	○	○	○	○	○
3	○	○	○	○	○	23	○	○	○	○	○
4	○	○	○	○	○	24	○	○	○	○	○
5	○	○	○	○	○	25	○	○	○	○	○
6	○	○	○	○	○	26	○	○	○	○	○
7	○	○	○	○	○	27	○	○	○	○	○
8	○	○	○	○	○	28	○	○	○	○	○
9	○	○	○	○	○	29	○	○	○	○	○
10	○	○	○	○	○	30	○	○	○	○	○
11	○	○	○	○	○						
12	○	○	○	○	○						
13	○	○	○	○	○						
14	○	○	○	○	○						
15	○	○	○	○	○						
16	○	○	○	○	○						
17	○	○	○	○	○						
18	○	○	○	○	○						
19	○	○	○	○	○						
20	○	○	○	○	○						

Interpreting Specs, Codes & Manuals

	A	B	C	D	E			A	B	C	D	E
1	○	○	○	○	○		21	○	○	○	○	○
2	○	○	○	○	○		22	○	○	○	○	○
3	○	○	○	○	○		23	○	○	○	○	○
4	○	○	○	○	○		24	○	○	○	○	○
5	○	○	○	○	○		25	○	○	○	○	○
6	○	○	○	○	○							
7	○	○	○	○	○							
8	○	○	○	○	○							
9	○	○	○	○	○							
10	○	○	○	○	○							
11	○	○	○	○	○							
12	○	○	○	○	○							
13	○	○	○	○	○							
14	○	○	○	○	○							
15	○	○	○	○	○							
16	○	○	○	○	○							
17	○	○	○	○	○							
18	○	○	○	○	○							
19	○	○	○	○	○							
20	○	○	○	○	○							

Communication - English

	A	B	C	D
1	○	○	○	○
2	○	○	○	○
3	○	○	○	○
4	○	○	○	○
5	○	○	○	○
6	○	○	○	○
7	○	○	○	○
8	○	○	○	○
9	○	○	○	○
10	○	○	○	○
11	○	○	○	○
12	○	○	○	○
13	○	○	○	○
14	○	○	○	○
15	○	○	○	○
16	○	○	○	○
17	○	○	○	○
18	○	○	○	○
19	○	○	○	○
20	○	○	○	○

Mathematics

1. A truck's fuel tank is 1/4 full. If the tank holds 120 litres total, how many more litres are needed to fill it to 3/4 full?

    a. 30 litres
    b. 60 litres
    c. 90 litres
    d. 45 litres

2. Subtract 3.45 from 10.

    a. 7.55
    b. 6.55
    c. 6.65
    d. 7.65

3. Which of the following is an improper fraction?

    a. 1/2
    b. 3/4
    c. 5/4
    d. 0.5

4. A piece of sheet metal weighs 2.4 kg per square metre. How much does a piece measuring 2 metres by 3 metres weigh?

    a. 4.8 kg
    b. 7.2 kg
    c. 12.0 kg
    d. 14.4 kg

5. Solve for x in the equation: 3x + 5 = 20.

    a. 5
    b. 8.3
    c. 15
    d. 3

6. A box of screws contains 250 units. If a project uses 80% of the box, how many screws are left?

    a. 200
    b. 50
    c. 80
    d. 170

7. What is the area of a triangle with a base of 10 cm and a height of 6 cm? (Area = 1/2 × base × height).

    a. 60 sq cm
    b. 30 sq cm
    c. 16 sq cm
    d. 20 sq cm

8. An apprentice earns $18.50/hour for the first 40 hours and "time and a half" for any overtime. If they work 44 hours in one week, what is their gross pay?

    a. $814.00
    b. $851.00
    c. $740.00
    d. $888.00

9. A driveway is 10 metres long and 3 metres wide. It needs to be covered in gravel 10 cm deep. How many cubic metres of gravel are required?

    a. 3.0 cubic metres
    b. 30 cubic metres
    c. 0.3 cubic metres
    d. 300 cubic metres

10. Convert 5 kilograms to grams.

    a. 50 g
    b. 500 g
    c. 5,000 g
    d. 0.005 g

11. Express 25% as a fraction.

    a. 1/4
    b. 7/40
    c. 6/25
    d. 8/28

12. 143 * 4 =

    a. 572
    b. 702
    c. 467
    d. 672

13. Express 125% as a decimal.

    a. .125
    b. 12.5
    c. 1.25
    d. 125

14. Multiply 10^4 by 10^2

    a. 10^8
    b. 10^2
    c. 10^6
    d. 10^{-2}

15. Solve for x: 30 is 40% of x

   a. 60
   b. 90
   c. 85
   d. 75

16. 12½% of x is equal to 50. Solve for x.

   a. 300
   b. 400
   c. 450
   d. 350

17. Express 24/56 as a reduced common fraction.

   a. 4/9
   b. 4/11
   c. 3/7
   d. 3/8

18. Express 87% as a decimal.

   a. .087
   b. 8.7
   c. .87
   d. 87

19. 60 is 75% of x. Solve for x.

   a. 80
   b. 90
   c. 75
   d. 70

20. 10 x 2 – (7 + 9)

    a. 21
    b. 16
    c. 4
    d. 13

21. 60% of x is 12. Solve for x.

    a. 18
    b. 15
    c. 25
    d. 20

22. Express 71/1000 as a decimal.

    a. .71
    b. .0071
    c. .071
    d. 7.1

23. 3^3 =

    a. $\sqrt{81}$
    b. 81/3
    c. 81
    d. 9

24. 4.7 + .9 + .01 =

    a. 5.5
    b. 6.51
    c. 5.61
    d. 5.7

25. .33 × .59 =

    a. .1947
    b. 1.947
    c. .0197
    d. .1817

Science

1. What is the primary purpose of a fuse or circuit breaker in a building's electrical system?

    a. To increase the voltage available to tools.

    b. To stop the flow of electricity if the current becomes too high and dangerous.

    c. To convert AC power to DC power.

    d. To store electricity for use during a power outage.

2. You are working with a chemical that has a high "reactivity" with water. What is the most important storage rule?

    a. Keep it in a clear glass jar.

    b. Keep it in a dry, moisture-free environment.

    c. Store it in a bucket of water to keep it cool.

    d. Always store it on the highest shelf.

3. A worker is using a 3rd class lever (like a shovel or a pair of tweezers). In this type of lever, the effort is applied between the fulcrum and the load. What is the main trade-off of this machine?

    a. It gives a great mechanical advantage in force.

    b. It requires less effort to lift a heavy load.

    c. It loses force but gains speed and distance at the load end.

    d. It is the most efficient lever for lifting rocks.

4. An air compressor tank fills up. As the air is pumped into the fixed volume of the tank, the pressure increases. If the temperature of the air also increases, the pressure will:

    a. Increase even more.

    b. Decrease because the air is thinner.

    c. Stay exactly the same.

    d. Force the air to turn into a liquid.

5. Which of the following is a sign of a chemical change (reaction) occurring?

    a. An ice cube melting.

    b. A piece of wood being sanded.

    c. A metal fence rusting.

    d. Water boiling in a kettle.

6. If you have a gear system where the drive gear has 10 teeth and the driven gear has 40 teeth, how many times must the drive gear turn to make the driven gear turn once?

    a. 1/4 turn

    b. 1 turn

    c. 4 turns

    d. 40 turns

7. A hydraulic system uses an oil with a specific viscosity. If the shop gets extremely cold over the weekend and the oil thickens, how will the system likely behave on Monday morning?

    a. It will move much faster due to the increased density.

    b. It will move slowly and sluggishly as the pump struggles to move the thick oil.

    c. It will stop working entirely because oil cannot flow when cold.

    d. The pressure will drop to zero.

8. What is the name of the central part of an atom that contains protons and neutrons?

    a. Electron cloud

    b. Shell

    c. Nucleus

    d. Orbit

9. You are looking at a "Health Hazard" WHMIS symbol (the person with the star on their chest). This product is likely to cause:

    a. Immediate death if swallowed.

    b. Chronic health effects like cancer or respiratory sensitization over time.

    c. A skin rash that clears up in an hour.

    d. An explosion if dropped.

10. A worker is heating a sealed aerosol can with a torch (which is very dangerous). Scientifically, why is the can likely to explode?

    a. The metal of the can becomes brittle when hot.

    b. The gas inside expands and the pressure increases until the can fails.

    c. The heat turns the gas into a solid, which takes up more space.

    d. The flame reacts with the paint on the outside of the can.

11. Which temperature scale is based on the freezing point of water being 0 degrees and the boiling point being 100 degrees?

    a. Fahrenheit

    b. Kelvin

    c. Celsius

    d. Rankine

12. In a parallel circuit with three light bulbs, if one bulb burns out, what happens to the other two?

    a. They both go out because the circuit is broken.

    b. They stay lit because they have their own paths to the power source.

    c. They get much brighter and then burn out.

    d. The fuse will blow immediately.

13. A contractor is choosing between two ramps to move heavy equipment into a trailer. Ramp A is 5 metres long and Ramp B is 8 metres long. Both reach the same height. Why is Ramp B the better choice for a very heavy load?

    a. It has a steeper slope, making the work faster.

    b. It has a gentler slope, providing a higher mechanical advantage (less force needed).

    c. It is shorter, so the equipment spends less time on it.

    d. It has less friction because it is longer.

14. You have two containers of the same gas. Container A is at 50 PSI and Container B is at 100 PSI. If both containers are the same size, which one contains more gas molecules?

    a. Container A

    b. Container B

    c. They both have the same number of molecules.

    d. It depends on the color of the containers.

15. What does a "Ground Fault Circuit Interrupter" (GFCI) outlet primarily protect a person from?

    a. High electricity bills.

    b. Electrical shock in wet locations.

    c. Dimming lights.

    d. Overheating of the wires in the wall.

16. A technician is working on a hydraulic brake system. They find that the brake pedal feels "mushy" and doesn't stop the car well. This is usually caused by air bubbles in the fluid. Why is air a problem in hydraulics?

    a. Air is too heavy for the pump.

    b. Air is compressible, while hydraulic fluid is not.

    c. Air makes the fluid too slippery.

    d. Air turns the fluid into a solid.

17. Which of the following is an example of a 1st class lever?

    a. A wheelbarrow

    b. A pair of scissors (the pivot is in the middle)

    c. A fishing rod

    d. A nutcracker

18. If an electric motor is rated for 120 Volts and it draws 10 Amps, what is the power consumption in Watts? (Power = Volts × Amps)

    a. 12 Watts

    b. 1,200 Watts

    c. 130 Watts

    d. 110 Watts

19. While inspecting a warehouse, you see a safety data sheet (SDS) for a chemical that says "Vapours are heavier than air." Where would this chemical be most dangerous if a leak occurred?

    a. Near the ceiling or roof vents.

    b. At chest height where people breathe.

    c. In low-lying areas like basements, pits, or sumps.

    d. Outside in the open wind.

20. Which simple machine is essentially an inclined plane wrapped around a cylinder?

    a. Bolt/Screw
    b. Wheel and Axle
    c. Pulley
    d. Gear

21. Which of the following is an example of torque?

    a. The wheel of a pulley turning
    b. A piston moving
    c. A horse pulling a load
    d. A tow truck pulling a vehicle

22. Find the weight of load L in N, if the pulling force F = 20N.

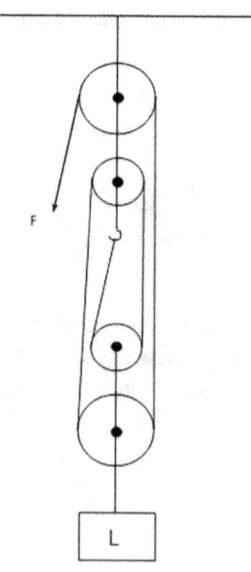

a. 5
b. 100
c. 20
d. 80

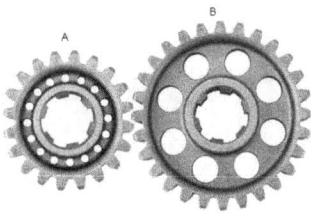

23. **How many turns does the gear B make when the gear A makes 14 complete turns?**

    a. 8
    b. 10
    c. 20
    d. 28

24. **Which of the following is true about the system of meshed gears shown?**

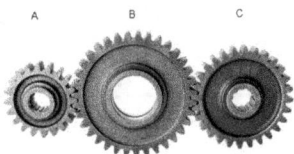

a. Gear A rotates slower than gear B
b. Gear A rotates slower than gear C
c. Gear B rotates slower than gear C
d. Gear B rotates faster than the other two gears

25. Which of the following is true of the relationship between screws and threads?

a. The larger the distance between threads, the easier to turn.

b. The smaller the distance between threads, the easier to turn.

c. The smaller the distance between threads, the more difficult to turn.

d. None of the above

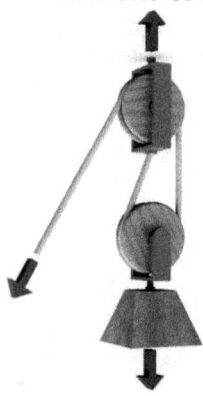

26. Consider the arrangement of pulleys above. If the weight shown is 150 pounds, how much force much be exerted to lift the weight?

a. 150 pounds
b. 100 pounds
c. 75 pounds
d. 50 pounds

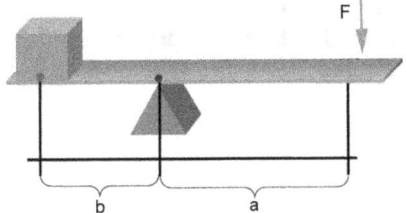

27. Consider the illustration above and the corresponding data:

Weight = W = 100 pounds
Distance from fulcrum to Weight = b = 5 feet
Distance from fulcrum to point where force is applied = a = 10 feet
How much force (F) must be applied to lift the weight?

    a. 100
    b. 50
    c. 25
    d. 10

28. Consider a gear train with 3 gears, from left to right, A with 10 teeth, gear B with 40 teeth, and gear C with 10 teeth. Gear A turns clockwise at 80 rpm. What direction and speed in rpm does Gear C turn?

    a. 100 rpm, clockwise
    b. 80 rpm clockwise
    c. 120 rpm counter clockwise
    d. 100 rpm counter clockwise

29. A force of 40 kg. is applied to two springs in parallel, which compresses the springs 10 inches. If the same force is applied to springs in series, how far will the springs compress?

   a. 40 inches
   b. 5 inches
   c. 10 inches
   d. 5 inches

30. Tension of 40 kg. is applied to two springs in series, which expand the springs 20 inches. If the same amount of tension is applied to springs in parallel, how far will the springs expand?

   a. 20 inches
   b. 10 inches
   c. 5 inches
   d. 2 inch

Interpreting Specs, Codes & Manuals

1. When a technician encounters a bolded "CAUTION" symbol in a manufacturer's manual, what does it primarily indicate?

   a. A mandatory requirement by the National Building Code
   b. A suggestion for improving the efficiency of the tool
   c. A potential hazard that could result in minor or moderate injury
   d. The specific location of the nearest emergency exit

2. Scenario: You are reviewing a Material Safety Data Sheet (MSDS) for a new degreaser. The "First Aid" section states: "In case of skin contact, flush with water for at least 15 minutes." A co-worker splashes a small amount on their arm. What is the correct immediate action?

    a. Apply a neutralising agent to the skin before rinsing
    b. Rinse the arm under a steady stream of water for the full 15 minutes
    c. Wipe the area with a dry cloth and wait to see if a rash develops
    d. Complete an incident report form before beginning the rinse

3. Scenario: A site blueprint includes the notation "N.T.S." in the bottom corner of a detail drawing for a staircase. How should you use this drawing?

    a. Use a carpenter's scale to determine the exact riser height
    b. Note that the drawing is Not To Scale and rely on written dimensions
    c. Assume the drawing is for a different project and discard it
    d. Standardize all measurements to the nearest metric equivalent

4. Scenario: You are reading a provincial electrical code manual regarding the installation of conduits. The manual states: "Conduits shall be supported at intervals not exceeding 1.5 metres, and within 300 mm of every outlet box." If you are installing a 4-metre run of conduit between two boxes, what is the minimum number of supports required?

    a. 2
    b. 3
    c. 4
    d. 5

5. A technical manual for a hydraulic lift specifies: "Check fluid levels bi-weekly or every 50 hours of operation, whichever comes first." If the lift was last checked on Monday after 10 hours of use, and it is now the following Thursday after an additional 45 hours of use, what should you do?

    a. Wait until next Monday to stay on the bi-weekly schedule
    b. Check the fluid level immediately because the hour limit was reached
    c. Add 5 hours to the clock before performing the check
    d. Skip the check since the machine is currently in use

6. In a Canadian workplace, what does the acronym WHMIS stand for?

    a. Workplace Hazardous Materials Information System
    b. Western Health Management and Industrial Safety
    c. Workers Handling Materials In Shippers
    d. Water and Heat Maintenance Integrated Specs

7. Scenario: You are reading the "Troubleshooting" section of a furnace manual. It says: "If the pilot light fails to ignite, ensure the gas valve is in the ON position and wait five minutes before attempting to relight." You find the valve is OFF. You turn it ON. What is your next step?

    a. Attempt to light the pilot immediately
    b. Wait five minutes to allow any accumulated gas to dissipate
    c. Call the manufacturer before touching the igniter
    d. Leave the valve OFF and report a mechanical failure

8. Scenario: A project spec sheet requires "304-grade stainless steel fasteners" for an exterior deck. You find a box of "Galvanized Zinc" screws that are the same size. According to the specs, can you use them?

    a. Yes, because galvanized screws are also rust-resistant
    b. No, because they do not meet the specific material grade required
    c. Yes, as long as you use twice as many screws for strength
    d. No, unless the temperature is expected to stay above freezing

9. Scenario: You are interpreting a site safety manual that lists "Mandatory PPE" for Zone A. The list includes: Hard hat, Steel-toe boots, and Safety glasses. A secondary note states: "Hearing protection required if noise levels exceed 85 decibels for more than 15 minutes." You are working in Zone A with a quiet hand tool for 4 hours. Which equipment is required?

    a. Hard hat, boots, and glasses only
    b. Hard hat, boots, glasses, and earplugs
    c. Only the hearing protection because of the duration
    d. None, since the tool is quiet

10. What is the primary purpose of a "Table of Contents" in a 500-page provincial building code book?

    a. To provide a summary of all recent legal changes
    b. To list the names of the engineers who wrote the code
    c. To help the reader quickly locate specific sections or chapters
    d. To define technical terms used throughout the document

11. Scenario: An equipment manual states: "Warning: Disconnect power source before removing safety guards." You need to clear a jam that is visible behind a mesh guard. The machine is plugged into a wall outlet. What is the most compliant action?

    a. Reach around the guard while the machine is idling
    b. Use a long stick to poke the jam while the power is on
    c. Unplug the machine from the wall before removing the guard
    d. Turn the "Off" switch on the machine but leave it plugged in

12. Scenario: A floor plan uses the symbol of a circle with a "T" inside it to denote a thermostat location. On the job site, you see a circle with an "S" inside it. Based on standard architectural symbols, what does the "S" likely represent?

    a. Smoke detector
    b. Storage closet
    c. Steel column
    d. Standard thermostat

13. Scenario: You are reading a spec for a concrete pour. It states: "Concrete must be maintained at a temperature of no less than 10°C for the first 72 hours. If ambient temperatures drop below 5°C, insulated blankets must be used." The forecast predicts a low of 3°C tonight. The concrete is currently 12°C. What action is required?

    a. No action is needed because the concrete is above 10°C
    b. Add hot water to the mix before the sun goes down
    c. Cover the concrete with insulated blankets
    d. Stop the pour and wait for a warmer week

14. In technical documentation, what does the term "Standard Operating Procedure" (SOP) refer to?

a. A set of step-by-step instructions to help workers carry out complex routine operations
b. The legal contract signed between a contractor and a homeowner
c. A list of all employees currently working on a specific job site
d. The total budget allocated for tools and machinery

15. Scenario: A manual for an air compressor states: "Maximum operating pressure is 120 PSI. Do not exceed 80% of maximum pressure for continuous use (longer than 30 minutes)." You need to run the tool for an hour. What is your target pressure?

a. 120 PSI
b. 100 PSI
c. 96 PSI
d. 80 PSI

16. Scenario: You are reading a fire safety code which states: "Fire extinguishers must be inspected monthly and tagged with the date of inspection." You find an extinguisher where the last date on the tag is January 15. Today is March 10. Is this extinguisher compliant?

a. Yes, because it is still within the same calendar year
b. No, because the February inspection is missing
c. Yes, as long as the pressure gauge is in the green zone
d. No, because tags must be replaced every week

17. Scenario: A workplace policy manual states: "In the event of a Category 1 gas leak, evacuate the building immediately. In a Category 2 leak, shut off the local valve and notify a supervisor." You smell a faint odour of gas near a single stove. According to the manual, a "Category 2" is defined as a localized leak with no immediate fire hazard. What should you do?

    a. Pull the fire alarm and run outside
    b. Shut off the stove's gas valve and find your supervisor
    c. Light a match to see where the leak is coming from
    d. Ignore it until the odour becomes stronger

18. What information is typically found in the "Glossary" section of a technical manual?

    a. A list of tools required for assembly
    b. Definitions of specialized or technical terms
    c. Contact information for the company's head office
    d. The warranty expiration date

19. Scenario: A blueprint shows a room dimension of 12' - 6". You are using a tape measure that only shows inches. What number are you looking for?

    a. 126 inches
    b. 144 inches
    c. 150 inches
    d. 156 inches

20. Scenario: A safety sign says "DANGER: High Voltage. Authorized Personnel Only." You are a first-year apprentice and need to retrieve a tool left inside that room. Your journeyman is currently off-site. What should you do?

    a. Enter quickly, as "Authorized" just means employees
    b. Wait for your journeyman or an authorized person to get the tool
    c. Call the police to report a locked room
    d. Proclaim yourself authorized for this specific task

21. **Scenario:** You are reading a manual for a chemical adhesive. It says: "Do not apply in temperatures below 15°C. Curing time is 24 hours at 20°C. For every 5 degrees below 20°C, double the curing time." It is currently 15°C. How long will it take to cure?

    a. 24 hours
    b. 36 hours
    c. 48 hours
    d. 72 hours

22. Which part of a manual would you check to find the specific part number for a replacement fan belt?

    a. The Index
    b. The Troubleshooting Guide
    c. The Parts List or Exploded View Diagram
    d. The Preface

23. **Scenario:** A set of specs for a plumbing job requires "Schedule 40 PVC pipe." You find "Schedule 80 PVC pipe" in the supply shed. You know Schedule 80 is thicker and stronger. What is the correct procedure?

    a. Use the Schedule 80 because it is an "upgrade"
    b. Check with the supervisor before substituting materials from the specs
    c. Use the Schedule 80 but charge the client for Schedule 40
    d. Cut the Schedule 80 pipe in half to match the thickness

24. **Scenario:** You are reading a work order that says: "Install 5 rows of tiles. Each row must have 8 tiles. Tiles are sold in boxes of 12." How many boxes must you open to complete the job?

    a. 3 boxes
    b. 4 boxes
    c. 5 boxes
    d. 40 boxes

25. Scenario: A site manual states: "All incidents resulting in property damage exceeding $500 must be reported to the Safety Officer within 2 hours." You accidentally back a truck into a fence. You estimate the repair will cost about $400, but the truck's taillight is also broken, which costs $150 to fix. What is your obligation?

    a. No report is needed because the fence is only $400
    b. Report the incident within 2 hours because the total damage is $550
    c. Wait until the end of the week to see if the boss notices
    d. Report it only if the fence owner complains

Communication - English

1. The old warehouse was designated as a hazardous area because of the presence of asbestos and lead paint. Designated means:

    a. Cleaned and renovated
    b. Officially assigned or identified
    c. Sold to a new owner
    d. Built many years ago

2. The safety inspector was known for being fastidious, often spending hours checking every single railing and ladder rung for even the slightest hint of a wobble. Fastidious means:

    a. Grumpy and hard to talk to
    b. Very attentive to and concerned about accuracy and detail
    c. Fast-moving and efficient on the job
    d. Likely to ignore minor mistakes

3. Despite the tight deadline, the supervisor insisted that safety protocols remain paramount, stating that no amount of saved time was worth a worker's life. Paramount means:

   a. Of secondary importance
   b. More important than anything else
   c. Equal to all other concerns
   d. Related to the budget

4. The lawyer argued that the contractor was liable for the damages because he had failed to install the proper drainage system as required by the local building code. Liable means:

   a. Responsible by law
   b. Likely to go bankrupt
   c. Exempt from punishment
   d. Skilled at a specific trade

5. To mitigate the risk of a fire during the welding process, a "fire watch" person was assigned to stand by with an extinguisher for thirty minutes after the work was finished. To mitigate means to:

   a. Ignore a potential problem
   b. Make something less severe or serious
   c. Increase the speed of a task
   d. Identify the cause of an accident

6. The ventilation fan was so loud it was deemed a nuisance by the office workers next door. What is the opposite of a nuisance?

   a. Distraction
   b. Benefit
   c. Requirement
   d. Hazard

7. The site safety audit revealed several superficial errors in the logbook, but the actual equipment maintenance was performed perfectly. What is a synonym for superficial?

   a. Dangerous
   b. Intentional
   c. Surface-level
   d. Significant

8. In an effort to be more frugal with the project budget, the foreman decided to repurpose leftover lumber from the previous job. What is an antonym for frugal?

   a. Wasteful
   b. Careful
   c. Generous
   d. Efficient

9. The inspector found that the ventilation in the paint booth was sparse, creating a risk for the workers. What is a synonym for sparse?

   a. Dangerous
   b. Thin
   c. High-quality
   d. Frequent

10. The structural integrity of the bridge was paramount to the safety of the surrounding community. What is an antonym for paramount?

    a. Vital
    b. Unimportant
    c. Primary
    d. Obvious

11. A supervisor asks for a "comprehensive" report on the day's progress. This means the report should be:

    a. Very short and written in bullet points
    b. Focused only on the mistakes that were made
    c. Complete and covering all necessary details
    d. Hand-written rather than typed

12. The site foreman states that the current ventilation system is "inadequate" for the fumes being produced. The foreman's primary concern is that:

    a. The system is too loud for the workers
    b. The system is using too much electricity
    c. The system is not good enough or sufficient for the task
    d. The system is too old and needs a warranty repair

13. During an assembly process, you are told that the parts must be "concentric." This describes parts that:

    a. Are made of the same alloy
    b. Share the same center point (like a pipe within a pipe)
    c. Are installed in alphabetical order
    d. Are designed to be discarded after one use

14. A contractor mentions that the soil at the excavation site is "unconsolidated." This suggests that the soil is:

    a. Frozen and impossible to dig
    b. Loose or not compacted, making it potentially unstable
    c. Contaminated with hazardous waste
    d. Owned by the municipal government

15. You are advised that a specific procedure is "prohibited" under current safety regulations. This means the procedure is:

   a. Optional depending on the site conditions
   b. The preferred method for experienced workers
   c. Strictly forbidden or not allowed
   d. Only allowed if a supervisor is watching

16. Choose the correct sentence:

   a. The manager gave the blueprints to Steve and I.
   b. The manager gave the blueprints to Steve and me.
   c. The manager gave the blueprints to I and Steve.
   d. The manager gave the blueprints to me and Steve.

17. Which word completes the sentence correctly? The permit was _____ than we expected to receive from the city.

   a. later
   b. latter
   c. latest
   d. late

18. Identify the correct use of a comma:

   a. After finishing the weld the technician cooled the metal.
   b. After finishing the weld, the technician cooled the metal.
   c. After finishing, the weld the technician cooled the metal.
   d. After, finishing the weld the technician cooled the metal.

19. The tools in the chest _____ to be cleaned and oiled.

    a. need
    b. needs
    c. is needing
    d. has needed

20. Which sentence is the most professionally written?

    a. If anyone has questions, they should see the foreman.
    b. If anyone has questions, he or she should see the foreman.
    c. If anyone has questions see the foreman.
    d. If anyone have questions, they should see the foreman.

Answer Key

Mathematics

1. B
Needs 1/2 tank. 120 / 2 = 60.
Common Trap: Option a is only a 1/4 tank increment.

2. B

3. C
Numerator is larger than denominator

4. D
6 sq m × 2.4 = 14.4

5. A
3x = 15; x = 5

6. B
20% remaining. 250 × 0.20 = 50

7. B
0.5 × 60 = 30

8. B
740 + [4 × 27.75] = 851

9. A
10 × 3 × 0.1 = 3
Common Trap: Option b assumes the depth is 1 metre instead of 10 cm.

10. C

💡 **Test Tip:** When dealing with measurement questions (like #29), always convert all units to the same format (e.g., convert cm to metres) before you start multiplying. It's the easiest way to avoid being off by a decimal point.

11. A
25% = 25/100 = 1/4

12. A
143 * 4 = 572

13. C
125/100 = 1.25

14. C
$10^4 / 10^2 = 10^{4+2} = 10^6$

15. D
40/100 = 30/X = 40X = 30*100 = 3000/40 = 75

16. B
12.5/100 = 50/X = 12.5X = 50 * 100 = 5000/12.5 = 400

17. C
24/56 = 3/7 (divide numerator and denominator by 8)

18. C
Converting percent to decimal – divide percent by 100 and remove the % sign. 87% = 87/100 = .87

19. A
60 has the same relation to X as 75 to 100 – so
60/X = 75/100
6000 = 75X
X = 80

20. C
10 x 2 – (7 + 9) = 4

21. D
60 has the same relationship to 100 as 12 does to X – so
60/100 = 12/X
1200 = 60X
X = 20

22. C
Converting a fraction to a decimal – divide the numerator by the denominator – so 71/1000 = .071. Dividing by 1000 moves the decimal point 3 places.

23. C
3^3 = 81

24. C
4.7 + .9 + .01 = 5.61

25. A
.33 × .59 = .1947

Science

1. B
Safety devices prevent fires by cutting power during overcurrent.

2. B
Water-reactive chemicals can explode or release toxic gas if they touch moisture.

3. C
Think of a baseball bat; you move your hands a little, the end of the bat moves a lot and very fast.

4. A
Pressure and Temperature are directly proportional in a fixed volume.

5. C
Rusting is oxidation, a chemical reaction that creates a new substance.

6. C
Driven (40) / Drive (10) = 4.

7. B
High viscosity means the pump has to work much harder.

8. C
The nucleus contains the mass (protons/neutrons).

9. B
The person symbol is for serious, long-term health risks.

10. B
Gas laws: Heat increases pressure until the container's structural limit is reached.

11. C
Celsius is the metric standard.

12. B
Parallel circuits provide multiple paths.

13. B
A longer ramp for the same height means a shallower angle and higher mechanical advantage.

14. B
Higher pressure in the same volume means more molecules are packed in.

15. B
GFCIs detect tiny leaks of current to ground and cut power in milliseconds.

16. B
Hydraulics rely on the fact that liquids don't compress. Air "gives" under pressure.

17. B
1st class: Load-Fulcrum-Effort (or Effort-Fulcrum-Load).

18. B
120 × 10 = 1,200.

19. C
Heavy gases sink and displace breathable air in low spots.

20. A
The threads of a screw are a spiral inclined plane.

Test Tip: On the Trades Science exam, always keep an eye out for "inverse" relationships. For example, in gears and pulleys, if you gain force (mechanical advantage), you always lose speed or distance. If an answer suggests you get both more force and more speed at the same time, it's almost certainly a distractor!

21. A
The wheel of a pulley turning is an example of torque. Torque, is the tendency of a force to rotate an object about an axis, fulcrum, or pivot. Just as a force is a push or a pull, a torque can be thought of as a twist to an object.

22. D
The block and tackle system composed of a system of pulleys as shown operates according the following rule:

Pulling Force=Load/(Number of supporting ropes)
Here, the number of supporting ropes is 4. So, we have
20 = Load/4
So, Load = 20 × 4 = 80 N.

Do not confuse the number of supporting ropes. The rope, which is being pulled, is not counted. Otherwise, you will obtain the wrong answer, Choice B 100 (20 × 5).

23. B
The equation of meshed gears states that the speed of rotation V (in rot/s) is inversely proportional to the number of teeth N. Mathematically,

$V_A/V_B = N_B/N_A$

From the figure, it is obvious that N_A = 20 and N_B = 28. So, we have

$14/V_B = 28/20$

$V_B = (14 \times 20)/28 = 10$ turns

24. C
In meshed gears, larger the gear, slower the rotation and vice versa. Thus, gear B rotates slower than the others and gear A rotates the fastest.

25. B
The smaller the distance between threads, the easier to turn.

26. C
75 pounds of force much be exerted downward on the rope to lift the 150 pound weight.

27. B
To solve for F, Weight X b (distance from fulcrum to weight) = Force X a (distance from fulcrum to point where force is applied)
100 X 5 = F X 10
500/10 = F
F =50

28. B
First calculate the speed of gear B. The gear ratio is 10:40 or 1:4. If gear A is turning at 80 rpm, then gear B, which is larger, will turn slower, 80/4 = 20 rpm.

Next calculate B and C. Gear C is smaller, so it will turn faster. The gear ratio is 40:10 or 4:1, and since gear B turns at 20 rpm, gear C will turn at 20 X 4 = 80 rpm.

Next calculate the direction. Gear A is turning clockwise, so Gear B is turning counter clockwise, so Gear C must be turning clockwise.

29. B
If the springs in parallel compress 10 inches, then the springs in series will expand half that amount, or 5 inches.

30. B
If the springs in parallel expand 20 inches, then the springs in series will expand twice that amount, or 10 inches.

Interpreting Specs, Codes & Manuals

1. C
In safety standards (ISO/ANSI), "Caution" is for moderate hazards. "Warning" is for serious injury, and "Danger" is for high risk of death.

2. B
Following the manual exactly is the core of "Reading Comprehension for Trades." Common Trap: Option (a) suggests a neutralizing agent, which is a common misconception that can actually cause chemical burns.

3. B
"N.T.S." stands for "Not To Scale." In trades, written dimensions always override the physical "scale" of a drawing.

4. B
You need a support within 300mm of each box (2 supports). The remaining distance is roughly 3.4m, which needs a support at least every 1.5m. Totaling 3 supports ensures no gap exceeds the limit.

5. B
"Whichever comes first" is the key phrase. Since 45 hours were added to the initial 10, the 50-hour limit (55 total) was passed.

6. A
This is a fundamental recall question for any Canadian tradesperson.

7. B
Safety manuals emphasize waiting to avoid gas explosions. Common Trap: Option (a) is the "rookie error" of rushing once the obvious problem (the valve) is fixed.

8. B
Specs are legal requirements. Substituting materials without approval is a breach of contract.

9. A
The noise hasn't reached the 85dB threshold, but the Zone A mandatory PPE still applies regardless of the task.

10. C
The Table of Contents is a navigational tool.

11. C
"Disconnect power source" means physical removal of the plug or locking out the breaker, not just turning a switch.

12. A
"S" in a circle is the standard symbol for a smoke detector/sensor. Common Trap: Option (d) assumes the shape (circle) is more important than the letter.

13. C
The manual gives a specific condition (ambient below 5°C). Since the forecast is 3°C, the blankets are mandatory.

14. A
SOPs ensure consistency and safety in a workplace.

15. C
80% of 120 is 96. (120 x 0.8 = 96).

16. B
"Monthly" means every month. If February is missing, the documentation is non-compliant.

17. B
Following the specific procedure for a "Category 2" leak as defined in the provided text.

18. B
Glossaries are for vocabulary and definitions.

19. C
(12 feet x 12 inches) + 6 inches = 144 + 6 = 150 inches.

20. B
Respecting "Authorized Personnel" signs is a critical safety and legal requirement in the trades.

21. C
15°C is 5 degrees below 20°C. The manual says to "double" the time (24 hours x 2 = 48 hours).

22. C
The parts list or "exploded view" shows how components fit together and their specific identifiers.

23. B
Even if a material is "better," it may not be compatible with other system components or the budget. Never substitute without permission.

24. B
5 rows x 8 tiles = 40 tiles. 40 / 12 = 3.33 boxes. You must open 4 boxes to have enough.

25. B
"Property damage" usually refers to the total cost of the incident ($400 + $150). Common Trap: Option (a) assumes you only count the damage to the other person's property.

Test Tip: When a question gives you a specific rule or definition (like the "Category 1 vs Category 2" leak), ignore what you think is common sense and follow the text exactly. The test is checking if you can follow a manual to the letter, not if you can guess what to do!

Communication - English

1. B (Officially identified).

2. B (Attentive to detail).
Common Trap: Choice C. The word sounds like "fast," but it actually means the opposite of "rushing" through a task.

3. B (More important than anything else).

4. A (Legally responsible).

5. B (Make less severe).
Common Trap: Choice D. Identifying a cause is part of a post-accident investigation, but "mitigating" is an action taken to prevent or lessen the impact beforehand.

Test Tip: When you see a word you don't know, try "The Substitution Trick." Replace the difficult word with each of the four options. Usually, three will sound clunky or change the meaning of the sentence entirely, leaving the correct one standing.

6. B
A nuisance is a source of annoyance; a benefit is a positive advantage.

7. C
Superficial means existing or occurring at or on the surface; not deep or thorough.

Option A is a common trap; while safety errors are bad, "superficial" means they didn't affect the core safety of the machine.

8. A
Frugal means sparing or economical with regard to money; wasteful is the opposite.

9. B
Sparse means thinly dispersed or scattered; not dense.

10. B
Paramount means more important than anything else; unimportant is the direct opposite.

Test Tip: For Antonym questions, always double-check if you are looking for the same or opposite meaning. A common mistake is picking a perfect synonym because it's the first word that "fits" the context, even though the question asked for the opposite.

11. C
Comprehensive means "all-inclusive."

12. C
Inadequate means it doesn't meet the minimum requirements.

13. B
Concentric refers to geometry where circles or cylinders share a center.

14. B
Unconsolidated soil is a major cave-in risk in trenching/excavation.

15. C
Prohibited means there is a "prohibition" or ban on the activity.

16. B
Use "me" as the object of the preposition "to." (Test: Remove "Steve" – "The manager gave the blueprints to me.")

17. A
"Later" refers to time. "Latter" refers to the second of two things.

18. B
Use a comma after an introductory phrase.

19. A
"Tools" is plural, so it takes "need."

20. B
"Anyone" is singular, so it requires a singular pronoun. "He or she" is grammatically precise.

TRADES SUPPLEMENTAL PRACTICE VAULT

Get the Competitive Edge
You've got the book, now get the reps in. Scan the code below or visit our site to unlock the Trades Supplemental Practice Vault. We've loaded it with over 600 additional practice questions—including Mechanical Comprehension, Spatial Relations, and two full-length "Final Exam" simulations.

https://courses.test-preparation.ca/course/trades-supplemental

Use Coupon Code: TRADES for 100% Free Access.

Because at the end of the day, we're here to make sure you pass.

The Essential Toolkit: Identification & Use

Measuring and Marking

- **Tape Measure:** The most used tool in the belt. In Canada, it's vital to have one with **both Metric and Imperial scales**, as we often design in one and build in the other.
- **Speed Square (Rafter Square):** A triangular marking tool used to layout 90-degree and 45-degree angles quickly. It also doubles as a fence for a circular saw.
- **Chalk Line:** Used for laying out long, straight lines over large distances, like a floor or a wall plate.
- **Torpedo Level:** A small level (usually 9 inches) with vials for checking 0° (level), 90° (plumb), and sometimes 45°. Essential for tight spaces.

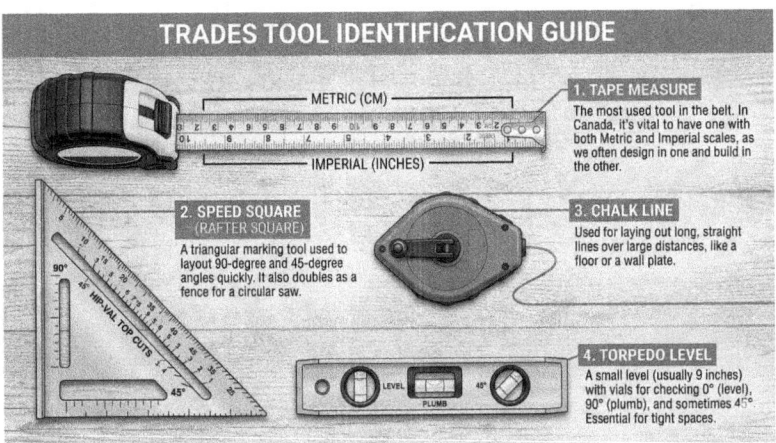

Cutting and Shaping
- **Utility Knife (Box Cutter):** Used for everything from opening material bundles to scoring drywall or trimming shims.
- **Wood Chisel:** A sharp metal blade used for carving or cutting away small amounts of wood, specifically for hinge recesses (mortises).
- **Handsaw:** While power saws do the heavy lifting, a fine-toothed handsaw is still the go-to for quick, precise manual cuts.
- **Hacksaw:** A fine-toothed saw designed specifically for cutting metal, such as copper pipe, conduit, or bolts.

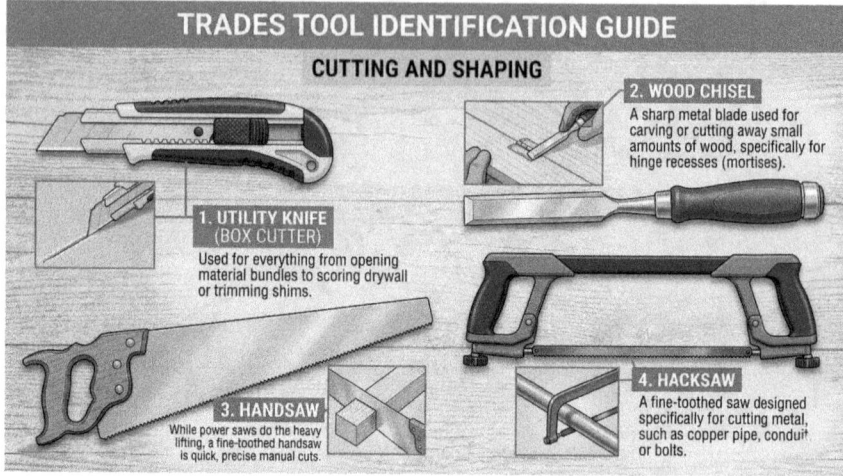

Fastening and Assembly

- **Robertson Screwdriver (Square Drive): The Canadian Classic.** Unlike the Phillips head, the Robertson has a square tip that doesn't slip easily. You'll need #1 (green), #2 (red), and #3 (black).
- **Claw Hammer:** The standard 16oz or 20oz hammer. The "claw" is for prying nails, and the "head" is for driving them home.
- **Adjustable Wrench (Crescent Wrench):** An all-purpose wrench with an adjustable jaw for turning nuts and bolts of various sizes.
- **Needle-Nose Pliers:** Used for gripping, bending, and cutting small wires, especially in electrical boxes or tight mechanical assemblies.

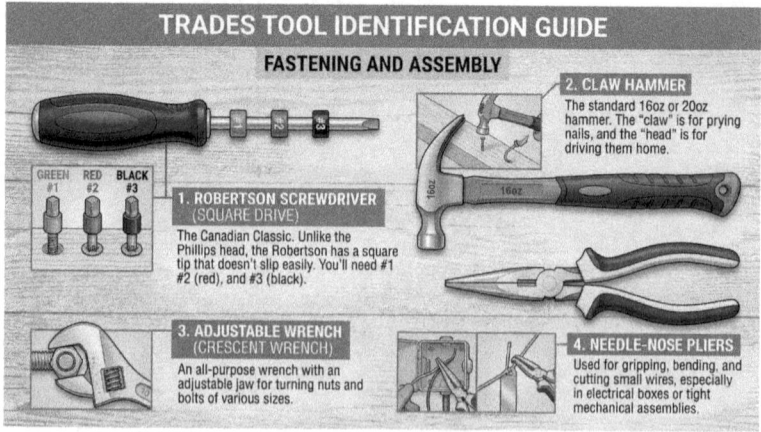

THE HIDDEN HURDLES: 10 REASONS GOOD STUDENTS FAIL (AND HOW YOU WON'T)

You can know your math and your mechanics inside out and still hit a wall on exam day. Over the years, I've seen students who were brilliant on the tools struggle with the test. Usually, it isn't a lack of brains—it's one of these ten "Red Flags."

1. The "Unit" Trap
In Canada, we live in a mix of Metric and Imperial. The exam loves to give you a problem in meters and ask for the answer in centimeters—or worse, mix the two.

- **The Fix:** Always circle the units in the question. If the math is easy, the trap is usually in the units.

2. Over-Thinking the Mechanical Logic
When you're looking at a diagram of a pulley or a lever, don't imagine a "real world" rusty machine.

- **The Fix:** On the test, pulleys have no friction and ropes don't stretch. Answer based on the physics laws in this book, not the stubborn crane you worked on last summer.

3. The "Rough Estimate" Mistake

In the trades, "close enough" can sometimes work. On a multiple-choice test, the examiners often provide "distractor" answers that are just slightly off from the correct calculation.

- **The Fix:** Do the full calculation. Don't pick the answer that "looks about right" until you've put pen to paper.

4. Mismanaging the Clock

People get stuck on one tough Algebra problem and spend ten minutes on it, leaving no time for the thirty easy questions at the end.

- **The Fix:** If a question takes more than 60 seconds, mark it, skip it, and move on. Come back to the "brain-teasers" once the easy points are in the bag.

5. Reading What You *Think* is There

Under stress, the brain skips words like **NOT**, **EXCEPT**, or **ALWAYS**.

- **The Fix:** Read the final sentence of the question twice before looking at the choices. Make sure you are actually answering what they asked.

6. Spatial Rotation "Dizziness"

Spatial relations (mental folding) can be exhausting for the brain. Students often give up halfway through the section because their "mental 3D camera" gets tired.

- **The Fix:** Look for "anchors." Find one unique side or a specific shaded corner and track only that piece as it rotates. Don't try to flip the whole object at once.

7. The "Second Guess" Syndrome

I've seen hundreds of exam papers where the student erased the correct answer and wrote down a wrong one.

- **The Fix:** Your first instinct is usually right. Unless you find a clear math error during your review, leave your first answer alone.

8. Neglecting the "Boring" Sections
Everyone studies the gears and the math, but many fail because they ignored the Reading Comprehension or Basic Science.

- **The Fix:** The exam is a total score. A point in Reading is worth just as much as a point in Advanced Algebra. Don't leave easy points on the table.

9. Falling for "Absolute" Language
In the trades, things are rarely "always" or "never" true. Test questions that use those words are often (but not always!) traps.

- **The Fix:** Be skeptical of answers that use extreme language. Look for the most balanced, logical choice.

10. The "Last Night" Burnout
The biggest reason for failure isn't a lack of study—it's a lack of sleep. Trying to cram 600 questions into your head at 2:00 AM the night before the test is a recipe for a "foggy" brain.

- **The Fix:** Treat your brain like a precision tool. It needs to be sharp. Stop studying by 8:00 PM the night before, eat a decent meal, and get some shut-eye.

The Finish Line (and Your New Start)

The Final Word
If you're reading this page, it means you've put in the hours. You've tackled the algebra, wrestled with the spatial relations, and worked through the mechanical problems that trip up most folks. That kind of diligence is exactly what's going to make you a great tradesperson.

Getting into a solid program or securing your apprenticeship is a massive milestone. The road ahead might have some grease on the gears and a few long days, but the reward—a career you can be proud of—is worth every bit of the sweat you've put into this book.

We've spent years at Complete Test Preparation triple-checking these questions because we know how much this exam matters to you. We don't just want you to pass; we want you to walk into that testing center with the confidence that comes from being truly prepared.

Study hard, get your reps in with the practice questions, and go claim your future.

Best of luck—we're pulling for you!

Keep the Edge: Free Updates & Extra Practice

Don't stop here. Requirements change and new tips come in from the field all the time. Register your book to stay in the loop and grab some extra practice while you're at it:

Register your purchase at:
https://test-preparation.ca/register/

By registering, you'll get the latest updates, our best test-taking strategies, and bonus practice questions delivered straight to your inbox.

Digital Toolbox

How to Prepare for a Test - The Ultimate Guide

https://www.test-preparation.ca/prepare-test/

Learning Styles - The Complete Guide

https://www.test-preparation.ca/learning-style/

Test Anxiety Secrets!

https://www.test-preparation.ca/test-anxiety/

Time Management on a Test

https://www.test-preparation.ca/time-management/

Flash Cards - The Complete Guide

https://www.test-preparation.ca/flash-cards/

Test Preparation Video Series

https://www.test-preparation.ca/test-video/

How to Memorize - The Complete Guide

https://www.test-preparation.ca/memorize/